Fresher PyQt5

A Beginner's guide to PyQt5

Edward Chang

Fresher PyQt5: A Beginner's guide to PyQt5

Edward Chang

Text copyright © 2020 by Edward Chang

All rights reserved. Without limiting the rights under the copyright reserved above, no part of this publication may be reproduced, stored in, or introduced into a retrieval system, or transmitted in any form or by any means (electronic, mechanical, photocopying, recording, or otherwise) without prior written permission.

For permission requests, please contact: @thehackeruni

ISBN: 9798615557859

Table of Contents

Preface ix
    1. Conventions used ix
    2. Book source code x
    3. Images x

Chapter 1: Your first PyQt programs 1
    1.1. First example 1
    1.2. Second example 4
    1.3. Summary 7
    1.4. References 7

Chapter 2: Layout management in PyQt 9
    2.1. Absolute positioning 9
    2.2. Layout classes 10
    2.3. Box layout 11
        2.3.1. Second example 12
        2.3.2. Third example 13
    2.4. Grid layout 15
    2.5. Form layout 16
    2.6. Summary 18
    2.7. References 18

Chapter 3: Signals and slots 19
    3.1. Custom slot 19
    3.2. Using a provided slot 21
    3.3. A typical example 23
    3.4. Summary 26
    3.5. References 26

Chapter 4. PyQt widgets 27
    4.1. QLineEdit 27
    4.2. QCalendarWidget 28
    4.3. QCheckBox 30
    4.4. QSlider 32
    4.5. QProgressBar 34
    4.6. QOpenGLWidget 37
    4.7. Miscellaneous widgets 41
        4.7.1. QComboBox 42

4.7.2. QMovie	42
4.7.3. QLabel	42
4.8. Summary	46
4.9. References	46
Chapter 5. FileLister	**49**
5.1. Qt Creator	49
5.2. Summary	58
Chapter 6: Currency Exchange Rates App	**59**
6.1. Designing the UI	59
6.2. Switching back to Python	60
6.2.1. Web service communication	61
6.3. Putting it all together	63
6.4. Summary	65
6.5. References	65
Chapter 7: PyQt databases and CSS styling	**67**
7.1. Qt Databases	67
7.1.1. Connecting to the database and querying it	67
7.2. Models	69
7.2.1. QsqlQueryModel	70
7.2.2. QsqlTableModel	72
7.2.3. QsqlRelationalTableModel	74
7.2.4. QSqlRelationalDelegate	78
7.3. CSS Styling	80
7.3.1. Style Rules	80
7.3.2. Selector Types	80
7.3.3. Sub-Controls	81
7.3.4. Pseudo-States	82
7.3.5. Conflict Resolution	83
7.3.6. Cascading	84
7.3.7. Inheritance	84
7.3.8. Example	86
7.4. Summary	91
7.5. References	91
Chapter 8: Radio App	**93**
8.1. Setting up	93
8.2. Gstreamer	94

8.2.1. Pipeline	95
8.2.2. Elements	96
8.2.3. Pads	98
8.2.4. Element states	98
8.2.5. Bringing it all together	99
8.2.6. Explanation of the code	102
8.3. Radio app	107
8.4. Summary	112
8.5. References	112
Appendix A: Multi-threading	113
A.1. How to implement threading	114
A.2. References	117
Appendix B: Network Access Manager	119
B.1. References	121
Appendix C: Setting up Cygwin	123
C.1. Initial setup	123
C.2. Your first package	124
C.3. Run the system for the first time	127
C.4. Installing additional packages	129
C.5. Packages to run basic scripts	130
C.6. OpenGL packages	132
C.7. Radio app	133

This page intentionally left blank

List of Figures

1.1. Your first PyQt app	4
1.2. Second example	6
2.1. Absolute positioning	10
2.2. Vertical box layout	12
2.3. Horizontal box layout	13
2.4. Horizontal and vertical combined	14
2.5. Grid layout example	16
2.6. Form layout	17
3.1. Custom slot demo	19
3.2. The LCD widget displays its default value	22
3.3. The LCD widget displays a new value based on the dial minimum	23
3.4. Your first interactive app	25
4.1. QLineEdit example	28
4.2. QCalendarWidget example	29
4.3. Programmatically toggle the calendar grid	31
4.4. Default slider orientation	32
4.5. Radio tuner simulation	34
4.6. QProgressBar demo	37
4.7. Output of the QOpenGLWidget demo on Cygwin	41
4.8. Jackpot!	45
5.1. Qt Creator	49
5.2. New file window	50
5.3. Form template selection	51
5.4. Make these adjustments	52
5.5. Pick a layout	53
5.6. Change attributes here	54
5.7. FileLister output	57
6.1. When you click the button, the text on the top 2 labels is cleared	60
6.2. Working with the requests module	61
7.1. Image courtesy of qt.io	71
7.2. QsqlTableModel demo	74
7.3. Lines 9 and 10 commented out	75
7.4. Line 10 commented out	76
7.5. Lines 9 and 10 both included	76

7.6. Using the QSqlRelationalDelegate class	78
7.7. Before applying CSS	86
7.8. After applying CSS	87
7.9. Eye candy	90
8.1. Is *gi* installed on your system?	94
8.2. Image courtesy of gstreamer.freedesktop.org	96
8.3. Data flows "down" the pipeline from left to right (image courtesy of gstreamer.freedesktop.org)	96
8.4. Image courtesy of gstreamer.freedesktop.org	97
8.5. First screen of your player	100
8.6. Select the file you created in the last section	101
8.7. The file is automatically played	101
8.8. Our radio app	107
A.1. Threads demo	113
C.1. The website	123
C.2. Mirror selection	124
C.3. Setup awaiting user input	125
C.4. Narrow down your choices	125
C.5. Choose the latest version	126
C.6. Error message	127
C.7. Start menu after installing xinit	128
C.8. Run this program	128
C.9. All GUI scripts should be run in this terminal	129
C.10. Confirm the installation of a package	130
C.11. Set up PyQt	131
C.12. The basic app	132
C.13. OpenGL error	132
C.14. widget5.py	133
C.15. Basic GTK setup on cygwin	134
C.16. Radio app on cygwin	134

Preface

I expected my first day in driving school to be easy. I imagined my instructor would slowly ease me into being a driver. Instead, I was shocked out of my illusion when my instructor informed me that he'd give me a lift back to my parents house. The only catch was that I would drive there.

I could bore you with a lot of theory about Python, the history of user interface (U.I.) design and so on. But, I trust that you'll be able to research all the dreary stuff when(if ever!) you need it. Instead, like Link in the Matrix, we'll skip all the boring stuff and get right to the meat and potatoes of the subject.

The only assumptions I make are:

1. That you're acquainted with the basics of Python. You can always refer to:
   https://docs.python.org/3/tutorial/
   if you're a bit rusty.

2. Some experience using the command line interface (CLI) on your operating system.

3. Know how to install python modules.

4. Basic knowledge of the HTTP protocol.

5. Basic knowledge of MySQL databases. A brief overview can be found at:
   https://www.tutorialspoint.com/sql/sql-overview.htm
   A beautifully designed e-book with more details can be found at:
   https://goalkicker.com/SQLBook/

It also helps to have experience with a "visual" programming language like Visual Basic, Delphi or mobile phone programming. But, it's not necessary.

1. Conventions used

There are a number of text conventions used throughout this book.

Italics: Used for a new term, an important word, or words, function names, variable names, command-line input and code in text. Here is an example:
Change the button from its default name *pushButton* to *btnBrowse*.

When we wish to draw your attention to a particular part of code or output, the relevant lines or items are set in bold: **Review the last minute of the video to see this!**

Tip

Tips and tricks appear like this.

Important

Warnings or important notes appear like this.

Note

Notes appear like this.

2. Book source code

Source code for the book can be found at:

https://gitlab.com/wohlstetter/freshr_pyqt5

3. Images

Some images had to be shrank so they could be displayed in the document. The most important of these can be found in the *images* folder of the source code.

So without further delay…

Hold on to your seat Dorothy, Kansas is about to go bye-bye!

Chapter 1: Your first PyQt programs

As at the time of writing this (February 14th 2020), the latest version of Python is version 3.8.1. I guess any version of Python 3 will work. Python 2 is great but won't work if you're using PyQt5.

Go to:

https://www.riverbankcomputing.com/software/pyqt/download5
download and install the latest version of PyQt appropriate to your operating system. It would be a good idea to make the binaries visible on your system path.

If you want to follow along, you can create a new text file and paste in the following code. Else, this and all other code will be found in the source code that came with your book. The code for each chapter is in a folder named after that chapter.

1.1. First example

In the folder for this chapter, open a file named *simple.py*.

```python
from PyQt5.QtWidgets import QApplication, QWidget  # 1
import sys  # 2

class MainWindow(QWidget):  # 3
    def __init__(self):  # 4
        super().__init__()  # 5
        self.initUI()  # 6

    def initUI(self):
        self.setWindowTitle('Simple example 1')  # 7
        self.resize(230, 254)  # 8
        self.show()  # 9


if __name__ == '__main__':  # 10
    qApp = QApplication(sys.argv)  # 11
    w = MainWindow()  # 12
    sys.exit(qApp.exec_())  # 13
```

Chapter 1: Your first PyQt programs

1 2 These lines import the modules needed to run the script. The function *exit()* that we'll later use to terminate our script is part of the *sys* module.

10 When the Python interpreter reads a source file, it executes all the code found in it.

Before executing the code, it will define a few special variables. For example, if the Python interpreter is running the source file as the main program, it sets the special __name__ variable to have the value "__main__". If this file is being imported from another module, __name__ will be set to the module's name.

In the case of our script, let's assume that it's executing as the main function, ie. you type something like

python simple.py

on the command line. After setting up the special variables, it will execute the import statement and load the modules specified in lines 1 and 2. It will then read the if statement and see that __name__ does equal "__main__", so it will execute the block shown there. Line 15 allows us to intercept the interpreter execution flow and harness it for our ends.

11 Every PyQt application must contain an instance of the application object. The *sys.argv* parameter contains a list of arguments passed to the script from the command line. In our case, we didn't pass any arguments to our script.

12 We instantiate an object called *w* from the *MainWindow* class. The *MainWindow* class contains all the functionality of our simple app.

13 We enter the main loop of the application. In programs with UI(user interface) components, whatever happens in the program for example if we resize the main window, drag objects into the main window is determined by actions the user makes.

Line 18 ensures that the execution flow loops infinitely while "listening" for user input. The event we're most interested in is the exit event, that is when the user closes the main window. We pass this to our script as its cue to terminate our script.

You may have noticed that our *exec()_* method has an underscore. This is because *exec* is a reserved Python keyword which we can't use.

So far we have looked at the script initialization boilerplate of our code. Now we examine the most important part of our simple script.

3 Here we define our main class which inherits from the *QWidget* class. This is why *QWidget* is passed as an argument to our class.

4 We called the init() method for our derived class on line 5. *super()* returns the parent object of our base class. Once we have this object, we call its init() method. This allows PyQt to perform its default initialization on our widgets.

5 We call the *initUI()* method. All our UI initialization is done in this method.

6 We declare the *initUI()* method.

7 Our widget in this example is our main window. We set the window title by calling the *setWindowTitle()* method and passing it the text we want to use as an argument.

8 The *resize()* method simply sets the size of a widget. We set a size of 230 pixels width and 254 pixels height.

9 We display our widget on screen. All UI components we interact with in PyQt for example buttons, sliders, drop-down menus etc are called widgets. The base class for all UI objects in PyQt is called QWidget.

Tip

The syntax for a derived class definition in Python looks like this:

```
class DerivedClassName(BaseClassName):
    <statement 1>
    ...
    <statement n>
```

To run the program, switch to the directory where the script is contained in your CLI. Type in the command:

python simple.py

Your output should look like this:

Figure 1.1. Your first PyQt app

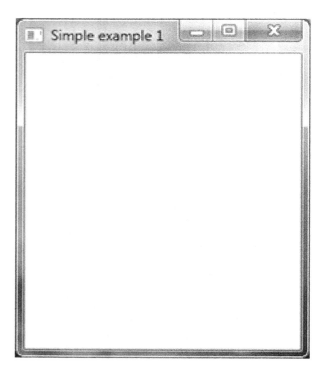

1.2. Second example

Look at the top-left hand corner of the illustration above! This is the generic icon which shows up in scripts run on Windows. You'll learn how to set up your own icon in the following script.

Open the file named *simple1.py*. Most of the code in this example was covered in the previous example. Let's go through what's new together.

```
 1 from PyQt5.QtWidgets import QApplication, QWidget,
QPushButton
 2 from PyQt5.QtGui import QIcon
 3 import sys
 4
 5 class MainWindow(QWidget):
 6     def __init__(self):
 7         super().__init__()
 8         self.initUI()
 9
10     def initUI(self):
```

```
11          self.setWindowTitle('Simple example 2')
12
13          self.setWindowIcon(QIcon('240px-Smiley.svg.png')) ❶
14
15          btnClick = QPushButton(parent=self) ❷
16          #btnClick = QPushButton(self)
17          btnClick.setText('Quit') ❸
18          btnClick.move(110, 50) ❹
19
btnClick.clicked.connect(QApplication.instance().quit) ❺
20
21          self.resize(300, 254)
22          self.show()
23
24
25 if __name__ == '__main__':
26     qApp = QApplication(sys.argv)
27     w = MainWindow()
28     sys.exit(qApp.exec_())
```

❶ We set an icon for our application. The *setWindowIcon()* method accepts a QIcon object as its argument. Of course, the file specified must exist or else Qt will fall back to the generic icon for your operating system.

❷ Here we create a button widget.

It's important to note that a widget without a parent widget is always an independent window, called a top-level widget. In the previous example, we worked exclusively with a top-level widget. Methods like *setWindowTitle()* and *setWindowIcon()* are only available to top-level windows.

Non-window widgets are child widgets, displayed within their parent widgets. Most widgets in Qt are mainly useful as child widgets. For example, it is possible to display a button as a top-level window, but most people prefer to put their buttons inside other widgets like we're doing on line 15.

You can declare a child widget like we have here on line 15 or you can do it as shown on line 16.

Please note that if you don't specify a parent for this widget, then it won't be visible on screen!

Chapter 1: Your first PyQt programs

3   We set the text property of our button. This is the text that will be seen on the surface of our button.

4   We position our button relative to our parent widget.

5   Here we set up code to handle user clicks on the button.

Android, Swift and many other "visual" programming languages, have callback functions to handle input events. Qt uses a signal and slot mechanism to handle input events.

In our case, a signal is emitted when the user clicks on the button we've created. A slot is code that processes this signal. A slot can point to a Python function or another slot.

The emitted signal is connected to the infinite loop which processes user events. The signal is connected to the quit() method which terminates the application. Communication is done between two objects: the sender and the receiver. The sender is the push button, the receiver is the application object.

To run the program, switch to the directory where the script is contained in your CLI. Type in the command:

python simple1.py

Your output should look like this:

Figure 1.2. Second example

1.3. Summary

This chapter walked you through installing PyQt as well as the basics of some very simple PyQt apps.

There is already a problem though: run *simple2.py* again to see it. The app as shown in Figure 1.2 has the button positioned roughly at the horizontal center of the screen. When you maximize the parent window, the button is pushed towards the top-left of the parent window. Try it for yourself and confirm this! The next chapter will teach you how to preserve widget positions regardless of parent window size.

1.4. References

- http://pyqt.sourceforge.net/Docs/PyQt5/class_reference.html

- https://docs.python.org/3/tutorial/classes.html

- https://stackoverflow.com/questions/419163/what-does-if-name-main-do

- https://stackoverflow.com/questions/18054720/what-is-callback-in-android

This page inten-
tionally left blank

Chapter 2: Layout management in PyQt

Layout management refers to the manner in which we position widgets on the application window. We can place our widgets using absolute positioning or with layout classes.

2.1. Absolute positioning

This is how we've positioned widgets so far. It has the following limitations:

- As shown before, the size and position of widgets don't change when we resize the parent window.

- Applications may look different on various platforms.

- If we change anything, we have to readjust the position of our widgets. A lot of precious developer time is wasted, getting everything just right.

The code below is contained in a file named *position.py* in the chapter 2 folder.

```
15 label1 = QLabel(parent=self)  ❶
16 label1.setText('Don\'t')
17 label1.move(80, 50)
18
19 label2 = QLabel(self)  ❷
20 label2.setText('use')
21 label2.move(90, 80)
22
23 label3 = QLabel('this positioning technique in real life!',self)  ❸
24 label3.move(100, 110)
```

❶ ❷ ❸ *QLabel* is used for displaying text or an image. Lines 15, 19, 23 show different ways of constructing the *QLabel* widget.

We position the labels by providing x and y Cartesian coordinates. The top-left corner of the parent window has coordinates (0,0) while the bottom-right corner has the maximum x and y coordinate values.

Figure 2.1. Absolute positioning

2.2. Layout classes

The Qt API(Application programming interface) provides layout classes for elegant management of widget positioning inside the container. The advantages of layout managers over absolute positioning are:

- Widgets inside the window are automatically resized.

- Ensures uniform appearance on display devices with different resolutions.

- Adding or removing widgets dynamically without having to redesign is possible.

Version 5.11 of Qt has 3 layout classes that we'll cover in this chapter:

- Box layout.

- Grid layout.

- Form layout.

2.3. Box layout

This layout is represented in Qt using the *QBoxLayout* class. This class lines up the widgets vertically or horizontally. Its derived classes are *QVBoxLayout* (for arranging widgets vertically) and *QHBoxLayout* (for arranging widgets horizontally).

The code below is contained in a file named *position1.py* in the chapter folder.

```
 9 def initUI(self):
10    self.setWindowTitle('Box layout1')
11
12    btn1 = QPushButton("Button 1", self)  ❶
13    btn2 = QPushButton("Button 2", self)  ❷
14
15    vbox = QVBoxLayout()  ❸
16    vbox.addWidget(btn1)  ❹
17    vbox.addStretch()  ❺
18    vbox.addWidget(btn2)
19    self.setLayout(vbox)  ❻
```

❶ ❷ These create two buttons and specify the text on them.

❸ A *QVBoxLayout* class lines up widgets vertically.

❹ Widgets inside a layout are displayed in the order in which they're added. Our layout will have 1 column with 3 rows. Line 16 adds *btn1* to the first row of the column.

❺ This adds a stretch factor or stretchable empty space between the two buttons.

❻ We set the layout of the main window.

Two buttons and a stretch factor are stacked vertically in the main window. The stretch factor will automatically take up the empty space between the two button widgets and the layout will ensure a consistent look on different window sizes.

Figure 2.2. Vertical box layout

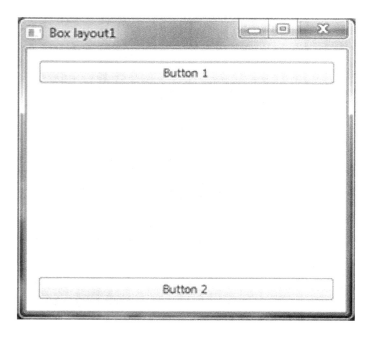

2.3.1. Second example

The code below is contained in a file named *position2.py* in the chapter folder. *QHBoxLayout* is used to stack the widgets horizontally from left-to-right.

```
 9 def initUI(self):
10   self.setWindowTitle('Box layout2')
11
12   btn1 = QPushButton("Button 1", self)
13   btn2 = QPushButton("Button 2", self)
14
15   hbox = QHBoxLayout()
16   hbox.addWidget(btn1)
17   hbox.addStretch()
18   hbox.addWidget(btn2)
19   self.setLayout(hbox)
```

Figure 2.3. Horizontal box layout

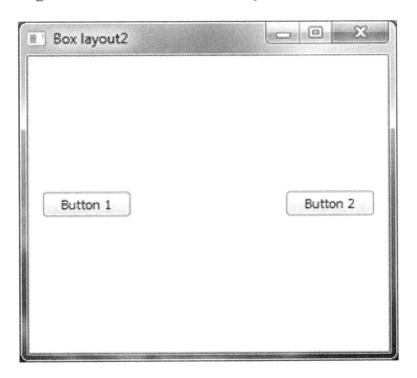

2.3.2. Third example

The code below is contained in a file named *position3.py* in the chapter folder.

```
 9 def initUI(self):
10   self.setWindowTitle('Box layout3')
11
12   btn1 = QPushButton("Button 1", self)
13   btn2 = QPushButton("Button 2", self)
14
15   vbox = QVBoxLayout()
16   vbox.addWidget(btn1)
17   vbox.addStretch()
18   vbox.addWidget(btn2)
19
20   btn3 = QPushButton("Button 3", self)
21   btn4 = QPushButton("Button 4", self)
22
23   hbox = QHBoxLayout()
```

```
24    hbox.addWidget(btn3)
25    hbox.addStretch()
26    hbox.addWidget(btn4)
27
28    vbox.addStretch()
29    vbox.addLayout(hbox)
30
31    self.setLayout(vbox)
32
33    self.show()
```

This example demonstrates nesting(i.e. one inside another) of layouts. First, two buttons with a stretchable empty space between them are added to vertical box layout. Then, a horizontal box layout object with two buttons and a stretchable empty space is added to it. Finally, a vertical box layout object is applied to the top level window using the *setLayout()* method.

Figure 2.4. Horizontal and vertical combined

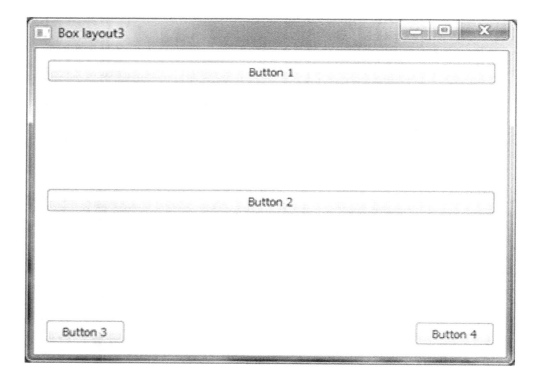

2.4. Grid layout

This layout is represented in Qt using the *QGridLayout* class. It is a grid of cells arranged in rows and columns. Coordinate 0,0 is at the left corner of the grid and the largest coordinate *x,y* depends on the width *x* and height *y* of the grid. The code below is contained in a file named *position4.py*.

```
10  def initUI(self):
11    self.setWindowTitle('Grid layout')
12
13    label1 = QLabel(self)
14    label1.setPixmap(QPixmap("Smiley_green_alien.svg.png"))  ❶
15    label2 = QLabel(self)
16    label2.setPixmap(QPixmap("Smiley_green_alien_wow.svg.png"))
17    label3 = QLabel(self)
18    label3.setPixmap(QPixmap("Smiley_green_alien_black_ninja.svg.png"))
19    label4 = QLabel(self)
20    label4.setPixmap(QPixmap("Smiley_green_alien_big_eyes.svg.png"))
21
22    grid = QGridLayout()
23    grid.addWidget(label1, 0, 0)  ❷
24    grid.addWidget(label2, 1, 0)  ❸
25    grid.addWidget(label3, 0, 1)  ❹
26    grid.addWidget(label4, 1, 1)  ❺
27
28    self.setLayout(grid)
29
30    self.show()
```

❶ I mentioned earlier that *QLabel* can display text or an image. Here, the *setPixmap()* method is used to point to this image. It accepts an argument of type *QPixmap*, so we pass a *QPixmap* object with the name of our image file as its constructor.

The label adjusts its size depending on the size of the *QPixmap* image.

❷ ❸ We put each label in a grid cell.
❹ ❺

Figure 2.5. Grid layout example

2.5. Form layout

This layout is represented in Qt using the *QFormLayout* class. This class is a conveniently lays out its children in a two-column form. The left column consists of labels and the right column consists of "field" widgets (line editors, spin boxes, etc.).

The code below is contained in a file named *position5.py*.

```
10 def initUI(self):
11   self.setWindowTitle('Form layout')
12
13   nameLineEdit = QLineEdit()  ❶
14   emailLineEdit = QLineEdit()  ❷
15   ageSpinBox = QSpinBox()  ❸
16
17   formLayout = QFormLayout()  ❹
```

```
18    formLayout.addRow("Name:", nameLineEdit)  5
19    formLayout.addRow("Email:", emailLineEdit) 6
20    formLayout.addRow("Age:", ageSpinBox)  7
21
22    self.setLayout(formLayout)
23
24    self.show()
```

1 2 We create two line edit fields. The *QLineEdit* widget is a one-line text editor. A line edit allows the user to enter and edit a single line of plain text with a useful collection of editing functions, including undo and redo, cut and paste, as well as drag and drop.

By changing its *echoMode()* method, it can also be used as a "write-only" field, for inputs such as passwords.

3 We create a spin box widget. The *QSpinBox* class provides a spin box widget. It is designed to handle integers and discrete sets of values (e.g., month names).

QSpinBox allows the user to choose a value by clicking the up/down buttons or pressing up/down on the keyboard to increase/decrease the value currently displayed. The user can also type the value in manually. The spin box supports integer values but can also be extended to use different strings with *validate()*, *textFromValue()* and *valueFromText()*.

4 5 6 7 Look at the figure below! To create such a layout we'd have created a vertical layout and nested three horizontal layout widgets inside it. Instead, by using *QFormLayout* each horizontal widget is added as a row. And we don't need to create label widgets, since this is automatically done for us. All we do is specify the text on the label plus its corresponding field element.

Figure 2.6. Form layout

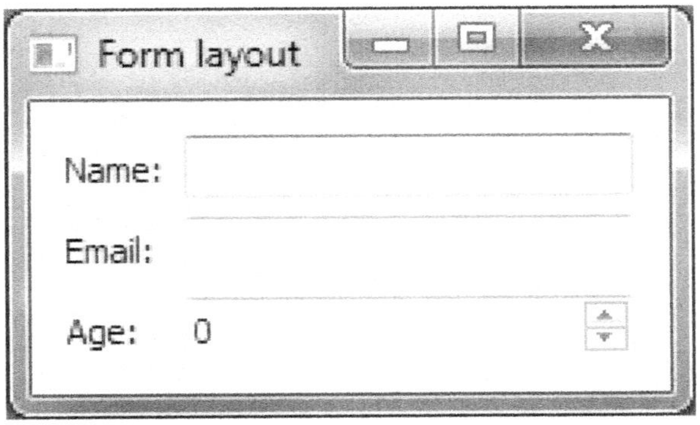

2.6. Summary

This chapter covered the basics of layout management. We briefly touched on event handling in the first chapter. The next chapter will further explore this topic.

2.7. References

- https://doc.qt.io/qt-5/qlabel.html#pixmap-prop

- https://doc.qt.io/qt-5/qhboxlayout.html

- https://doc.qt.io/qt-5/qvboxlayout.html

- https://doc.qt.io/qt-5/qformlayout.html

- https://doc.qt.io/qt-5/qspinbox.html

- https://doc.qt.io/qt-5/qlineedit.html

Chapter 3: Signals and slots

As mentioned in chapter one, Qt uses a signal and slot mechanism to handle input events. A signal is emitted when something of potential interest happens. A slot is a Python callable(think of this as a function). If a signal is connected to a slot then the slot is called when the signal is emitted. If a signal isn't connected then nothing happens.

For example, the spinbox in *position5.py* emits a signal whenever you move the slider up or down. But since it wasn't connected to a slot, Qt ignores the signal. Have a look at:

https://doc.qt.io/qt-5/qspinbox.html#valueChanged

In addition to notifying Qt that the spin box has been clicked on, the spin object also passes data about the current value of the spin box. Usually as a coder all you're interested in is the click event. The code listing below shows you how to use this extra data in case you ever need it.

3.1. Custom slot

The code below is contained in a file named *signals.py* in the chapter folder. Run the script and pay close attention to your CLI window. When you click the up or down arrows on the spin box, the current value of the spin box is printed to your CLI.

Figure 3.1. Custom slot demo

```
1 from PyQt5.QtWidgets import QApplication, QWidget,
  QFormLayout, QSpinBox, QLineEdit
2 from PyQt5.QtCore import pyqtSlot ❶
3 import sys
```

```
 4
 5  class MainWindow(QWidget):
 6      def __init__(self):
 7          super().__init__()
 8          self.initUI()
 9
10
11      def initUI(self):
12          self.setWindowTitle('Signals example')
13
14          nameLineEdit = QLineEdit()
15          emailLineEdit = QLineEdit()
16          ageSpinBox = QSpinBox()
17
18          formLayout = QFormLayout()
19          formLayout.addRow("Name:", nameLineEdit)
20          formLayout.addRow("Email:", emailLineEdit)
21          formLayout.addRow("Age:", ageSpinBox)
22
23          ageSpinBox.valueChanged[int].connect(self.headsUp)  ❷
24
25          self.setLayout(formLayout)
26
27          self.show()
28
29      @pyqtSlot(int)  ❸
30      def headsUp(self, arg1):  ❹
31          print("New value is", arg1)  ❺
32
33  if __name__ == '__main__':
34      qApp = QApplication(sys.argv)
35      w = MainWindow()
36      sys.exit(qApp.exec_())
```

❶ We need to import this module in order to use the *pyqtSlot* decorator. For more information on decorators see:

https://gist.github.com/Zearin/2f40b7b9cfc51132851a

https://realpython.com/primer-on-python-decorators/

2 As explained in the documentation for *QSpinBox*, this widget can emit a value changed signal, that contains integer data. Line 23, shows PyQt syntax for registering a slot for this signal and its data.

3 Although PyQt5 allows any Python callable to be used as a slot when connecting signals, it is sometimes necessary to explicitly mark a Python method as being a Qt slot and to provide a C++ signature for it. PyQt5 provides the *pyqtSlot()* function decorator to do this. Line 29 declares a slot that processes integer values.

4 We declare a function that will take one integer parameter called *arg1*.

5 We print our value on the command prompt.

Important

The *pyqtSlot()* function decorator syntax is:

PyQt5.QtCore.pyqtSlot(types[, name[, result[, revision=0]]])

Where:

types – the types that define the C signature of the slot. Each type may be a Python type object or a string that is the name of a C type.

name – the name of the slot that will be seen by C++. If omitted the name of the Python method being decorated will be used. This may only be given as a keyword argument.

revision – the revision of the slot that is exported to QML. This may only be given as a keyword argument.

result – the type of the result and may be a Python type object or a string that specifies a C++ type. This may only be given as a keyword argument.

3.2. Using a provided slot

The previous example showed you how to create a custom slot to process widget signals. However, most widgets already come with some slots built in.

The code below is contained in a file named *signals1.py*.

```
 9 def initUI(self):
10   self.setWindowTitle('Signals example1')
11
```

Chapter 3: Signals and slots 22

```
12   lcd = QLCDNumber(self)  ❶
13   dial = QDial(self)  ❷
14   dial.setMinimum(50)  ❸
15
16   vbox = QVBoxLayout()
17   vbox.addWidget(lcd)
18   vbox.addWidget(dial)
19
20   self.setLayout(vbox)
21   dial.valueChanged.connect(lcd.display)  ❹
```

❶ ❷ We display a *QDial* which looks like a knob on an analogue device and a *QLCDNumber* display widget. *QDial* is used when the user needs to control a value within a program-definable range, and the range either wraps around (for example, with angles measured from 0 to 359 degrees). The *QLCDNumber* widget displays a number with LCD-like digits.

❸ We set a minimum value for our dial.

❹ We connect the *valueChanged* signal of the slider to the display slot of the LCD widget. It will display whatever is emitted from the dial.

When you first run the script, the LCD will display a default value of 0.

Figure 3.2. The LCD widget displays its default value

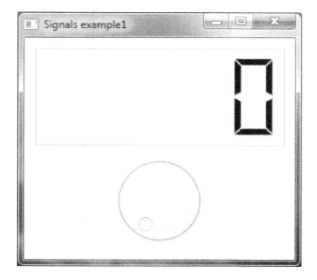

When you move the slider **slightly**, a signal is sent to the LCD which sets its minimum value to 50.

Figure 3.3. The LCD widget displays a new value based on the dial minimum

3.3. A typical example

Usually, all your interested in is the click event. The example below shows the pattern of most PyQt scripts you'll encounter. Its code is contained in a file named *signal2.py*.

```
 9  def initUI(self):
10      self.setWindowTitle('Signals example2')
11
12      self.nameLineEdit = QLineEdit()
13      self.submitButton = QPushButton("&Submit")
14
15      formLayout = QFormLayout()
16      formLayout.addRow("Name:", self.nameLineEdit)
17
18      vbox = QVBoxLayout()
19      vbox.addLayout(formLayout)
20      vbox.addWidget(self.submitButton)
21
22      self.submitButton.clicked.connect(self.submitContact)  ❶
23
24      self.setLayout(vbox)
25      self.show()
```

```
26
27  def submitContact(self):
28      name = self.nameLineEdit.text()  ❷
29
30      if name == "":  ❸
31          QMessageBox.critical(self, "Empty Field",
32                  "Please enter a name!")  ❹
33      else:
34          QMessageBox.information(self, "Success!",
35                  "Hello %s!" % name)
```

❶ Most of this code is familiar to you. We nest a form layout inside a vertical box layout. Line 22 forwards the click signal on the button to the *submitContact()* method.

❷ We're inside the *submitContact()* method. We retrieve the value of the line edit widget and assign it to a variable called *name*.

❸ ❹ If the line edit widget is blank we issue an error message. The first parameter on line 31 refers to the parent window. The second is the text shown in the title of the message box. The third parameter is the main text of the message box. We show a message box with a critical severity level.

Important

The *QMessageBox* class provides a modal dialog for informing the user or for asking the user a question and receiving an answer. It has four predefined message severity levels, or message types, which really only differ in the predefined icon they each show. These are:

1. **Question**: For asking a question during normal operations.

2. **Information**: For reporting information about normal operations.

3. **Warning**: For reporting non-critical errors.

4. **Critical**: For reporting critical errors.

Figure 3.4. Your first interactive app

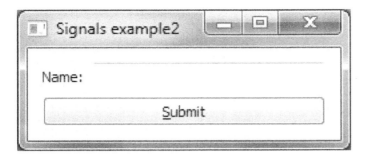

3.4. Summary

This chapter introduced PyQt signals and slots to you. Interacting with your users will usually be the core of your PyQt apps and signals will help you with this. Most widgets provide easy to use signals and slots. The Qt documentation will be a great help as you write more complex apps.

Of course, more complex programs use a U.I. designer. The next chapter will introduce PyQt's visual design program as well as a more useful app.

3.5. References

- https://doc.qt.io/qt-5/qabstractslider.html#minimum-prop

- https://doc.qt.io/qt-5/qmessagebox.html#details

- http://pyqt.sourceforge.net/Docs/PyQt5/signals_slots.html

Chapter 4. PyQt widgets

Let's review some widgets you're likely to encounter while coding with PyQt.

4.1. QLineEdit

By now, you're well acquainted with this one. The *QLineEdit* widget is a one-line text editor. A line edit allows the user to enter and edit a single line of plain text with a useful collection of editing functions, including undo and redo, cut-and-paste, as well as drag and drop.

Have a look at the following snippet from *widgets.py*!

```
11 def initUI(self):
12   self.setWindowTitle('QLineEdit widget')
13
14   basicLineEdit = QLineEdit(self)
15   self.resultLabel = QLabel(self)
16
17   basicLineEdit.move(10,100)
18   #self.resultLabel.setMaximumWidth(100)
19   self.resultLabel.move(10,150)
20
21   basicLineEdit.textChanged[str].connect(self.headsUp)  [1]
22
23   self.resize(300, 300)
24   self.show()
25
26 @pyqtSlot(str)  [2]
27 def headsUp(self, arg1):
28   self.resultLabel.setText(arg1)  [3]
29   self.resultLabel.adjustSize()  [4]
```

[1] We connect the *textChanged* signal emitted by the widget to our slot. Any time you alter, the text within a *QLineEdit*, this signal is emitted. The emitted signal has an argument of type string, which contains the text contained in the widget.

[2] We declare a slot that processes values of type string.

[3] We take the value of the line edit widget and set it as the text for the label.

4 This will adjust the width of the label widget to match the text contained in it. It's quite possible for a *QLabel* widget to contain more text than is displayed on its face. Don't believe me? Un-comment line 18 and run the app again! The label will only display 100 pixels of text.

Figure 4.1. QLineEdit example

4.2. QCalendarWidget

The *QCalendarWidget* class provides a monthly based calendar widget allowing the user to select a date. By default, the current date is selected, and the user can select another date using both mouse and keyboard. The calendar grid is not visible by default.

If we select a date on the widget, a *clicked* signal is emitted. The code contained in *widget1.py* connects this signal to our custom slot.

```
11  def initUI(self):
12    self.setWindowTitle('QCalendarWidget example')
13
14    vbox = QVBoxLayout(self)
15
16    calendar = QCalendarWidget(self)
17    calendar.setGridVisible(True)  １
18    calendar.clicked[QDate].connect(self.headsUp)
19
```

```
20    self.resultLabel =
QLabel(calendar.selectedDate().toString(),self) ▧
21
22    vbox.addWidget(calendar)
23    vbox.addWidget(self.resultLabel)
24
25    self.resize(300, 300)
26    self.show()
27
28  @pyqtSlot(QDate)
29  def headsUp(self, arg1):
30    self.resultLabel.setText(arg1.toString()) ▧
```

▧   This enables the calendar grid.

▧   *calendar.selectedDate()* returns an object of type *QDate*. Since the label widget only accepts string objects, we call the *toString()* method of *QDate* to convert the output into a format acceptable by our label widget. When the app is first run, the label will display the current date.

▧   When we select any date on our calendar, a signal containing the chosen date is emitted. We capture that date and display it on our label.

Figure 4.2. QCalendarWidget example

4.3. QCheckBox

A *QCheckBox* is an option button that can be switched on (checked) or off (unchecked). Checkboxes are typically used to represent features in an application that can be enabled or disabled without affecting others.

Whenever a checkbox is checked or cleared, it emits the signal *stateChanged()*. The code contained in *widget2.py* connects to this signal. We use it to toggle the grid on the calendar widget.

```
11 def initUI(self):
12   self.setWindowTitle('QCheckBox example')
13
14   vbox = QVBoxLayout(self)
15
16   self.calendar = QCalendarWidget(self)
17   self.calendar.setGridVisible(True)
18   self.calendar.clicked[QDate].connect(self.headsUp)
19
20   checkbox = QCheckBox('Disable Grid?', self)  ❶
21   #checkbox.stateChanged.connect(self.toggleCalendarGrid)
22   checkbox.stateChanged.connect(self.headsUp)  ❷
23
24   self.resultLabel = QLabel(self.calendar.selectedDate().toString(),self)
25
26   vbox.addWidget(checkbox)
27   vbox.addWidget(self.calendar)
28   vbox.addWidget(self.resultLabel)
29
30   self.resize(300, 300)
31   self.show()
32
33 @pyqtSlot(QDate)
34 def headsUp(self, arg1):
35   self.resultLabel.setText(arg1.toString())
36
```

```
37 @pyqtSlot()
38 def headsUp(self):
39   if not (self.calendar.isGridVisible()): ❸
40     self.calendar.setGridVisible(True) ❹
41   else:
42     self.calendar.setGridVisible(False) ❺
```

❶   We construct the checkbox widget and set its text.
❷   We connect the *stateChanged()* signal to our slot.
❸ ❹ By default the calendar grid is enabled. If the user checks the checkbox, the grid will be disabled if it's currently enabled.
❺   Vice-versa.

> **Note**
> Did you notice that both slots have the same name? Depending on the arguments passed to it, the interpreter will appropriately determine which slot to use when handling a signal.

Figure 4.3. Programmatically toggle the calendar grid

Instead of using a slot, we can also use a callback function to produce similar output. The function *toggleCalendarGrid()* in *widget2.py* demonstrates this. When you're not interested in processing parameters from our widgets, one may use a callback. The PyQt documentation at:

http://pyqt.sourceforge.net/Docs/PyQt5/signals_slots.html#the-pyqtslot-decorator

indicates that slots reduce the amount of memory used and are faster.

4.4. QSlider

The QSlider widget provides a vertical or horizontal slider. The slider is the classic widget for controlling a bounded value. It lets the user move a slider handle along a horizontal or vertical groove and translates the handle's position into an integer value within the legal range.

By default, the slider is oriented vertically:

Figure 4.4. Default slider orientation

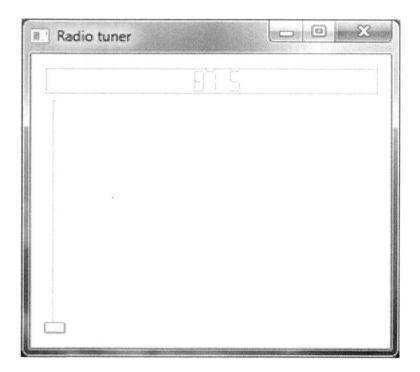

The code contained in *widget3.py* will show you how to change the slider orientation. We use a slider together with a *QLCDNumber* widget to simulate a radio tuner.

```
10  def initUI(self):
11      self.setWindowTitle('Radio tuner')
12
13      self.lcd = QLCDNumber(self)
14      slider = QSlider(self)
15      slider.setOrientation(Qt.Horizontal) ❶
```

```
16    self.lcd.setProperty("value", 87.5) ❷
17
18    vbox = QVBoxLayout()
19    vbox.addWidget(self.lcd)
20    vbox.addWidget(slider)
21
22    self.setLayout(vbox)
23    slider.valueChanged[int].connect(self.headsUp) ❸
24
25    self.resize(300, 254)
26    self.show()
27
28 @pyqtSlot(int)
29 def headsUp(self, arg1):
30    display = str(87.5 + (0.205*arg1)) ❹
31    self.lcd.setProperty("value", display)
```

❶ As mentioned earlier, the default slider orientation is vertical. The slider widgets alternate orientation can be set using the *setOrientation()* method as shown here. We pass it an enumerated value of *Qt.Horizontal*.

❷ This demonstrates setting the default display value for the LCD widget.

❸ The slider emits a *valueChanged* signal when its value has changed. The default slider range is between 0 and 99. Whenever you move this slider, it calculates how far within its range you've moved it and emits a signal containing its new position(as an integer) within the range. Please note that the slider can only handle integer values! We take advantage of that in our custom slot.

❹ Many countries use an FM broadcast band range of 87.5 to 108 MHz. Subtract 87.5 from 108 to get 20.5. Then divide that by 100 to get a step size of 0.205. Every time you shift the slider, the script takes its current position between 0 and 99 and calculates the corresponding frequency using the formula shown on this line.

Figure 4.5. Radio tuner simulation

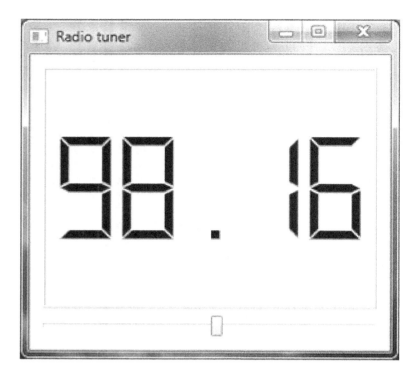

4.5. QProgressBar

The *QProgressBar* widget provides a horizontal(by default) or vertical progress bar. The progress bar uses the concept of steps. You set it up by specifying the minimum and maximum possible step values, and it will display the percentage of steps that have been completed when you later give it the current step value.

The default minimum is 0, default maximum is 99 and the default step size is 1. *QProgressBar* utilizes animation to give the illusion of ticking away.

The code contained in *widget4.py* simulates a download or file transfer progress bar.

```
1 from PyQt5.QtWidgets import QApplication, QWidget, QPushButton, QProgressBar
2 from PyQt5.QtCore import pyqtSlot, QTimeLine
3 import sys
4
5 class MainWindow(QWidget):
6     def __init__(self):
```

```
 7            super().__init__()
 8            self.initUI()
 9
10
11      def initUI(self):
12            self.setWindowTitle('QProgressBar demo')
13
14            self.timerButton = QPushButton("Start", self)
15            self.timerButton.clicked.connect(self.timerStart)
16
17            self.progressBar = QProgressBar(self) ❶
18            self.progressBar.setGeometry(10, 20, 290, 25) ❷
19
20            self.timerObject = QTimeLine(2000, self) ❸
21            self.timerObject.setFrameRange(0, 100) ❹
22            self.timerObject.finished.connect(lambda: self.timerButton.setText("Finished")) ❺
23            self.timerObject.frameChanged.connect(self.progressBar.setValue) ❻
24
25            self.timerButton.move(110,150)
26            self.progressBar.move(10,100)
27
28            self.resize(300, 300)
29            self.show()
30
31      @pyqtSlot()
32      def timerStart(self):
33            if (self.timerObject.state() == QTimeLine.Running): ❼
34                  self.timerObject.stop() ❽
35                  self.timerButton.setText("Resume") ❾
36            else:
37                  self.timerButton.setText("Pause") ❿
38                  self.timerObject.resume() ⓫
```

1 2 We initialize our progress bar widget. We also set its dimensions by specifying its top-left and bottom-right corners.

3 As mentioned earlier, the progress bar uses animation. The *QTimeLine* class provides a timeline for controlling animations. We use it here to animate the progress bar widget by calling a slot periodically.

This line calls constructs a 2000 millisecond(2 seconds) timeline.

4 We set the frame range for our *QTimeLine* object. Every 2000/100 milliseconds, it will move to the next frame of the animation.

5 When the timeline object finishes its count, it will emit a *finished* signal. We connect this signal to a lambda function that changes the label on the button.

6 Every time the frame changes a signal is emitted that contains the integral value of the new frame. We take this integer and use it to set the new value of the progress bar widget.

7 8 This slot is called whenever the user clicks on the button in the app. If we click on the button
9 while the timer is still running, the timer will pause and the text on the button is changed to "Resume".

10 If the timer is still running and is currently paused, we resume the timer and change the button
11 text to "Pause".

Tip

Lambdas are one line functions. They are also known as anonymous functions in some languages. You use lambdas when you don't want to call a function twice in a program. They are just like normal functions and even behave like them.

The general form of a lambda function is:

```
lambda argument: manipulate(argument)
```

For example:

```
add = lambda x, y: x + y
```

when you call

```
print(add(1, 9))
```

you'll get

Figure 4.6. QProgressBar demo

4.6. QOpenGLWidget

QOpenGLWidget provides functionality for displaying OpenGL graphics integrated into a Qt application. It is very simple to use: Make your class, inherit from it and use the subclass like any other *QWidget*, except that you have the choice between using *QPainter* and standard OpenGL rendering commands.

QOpenGLWidget provides three convenient virtual functions that you can re-implement in your subclass to perform the typical OpenGL tasks:

1. *paintGL()* - Renders the OpenGL scene. Gets called whenever the widget needs to be updated.
2. *resizeGL()* - Sets up the OpenGL viewport, projection, etc. Gets called whenever the widget has been resized (and also when it is shown for the first time because all newly created widgets get a resize event automatically).
3. *initializeGL()* - Sets up the OpenGL resources and state. Gets called once before *resizeGL()* or *paintGL()* are called.

Chapter 4. PyQt widgets

A comprehensive overview of OpenGL is beyond the scope of this document. Our focus will be on the interaction of this widget with PyQt. An app in a later chapter will use this widget (although it won't use any OpenGL code). A good beginner guide from the developers of OpenGL can be found at:

https://www.khronos.org/opengl/wiki/Getting_Started

Tip

You'll probably need to install PyOpenGL to get the code below to run. Run the following command to install it:

pip3 install PyOpenGL PyOpenGL_accelerate

See:

http://pyopengl.sourceforge.net/documentation/installation.html

for more details.

For Windows users, you may refer to Appendix C for instructions on how to set up OpenGL on cygwin.

The code contained in *widget5.py* draws a cube using OpenGL.

```
 1 from PyQt5.QtWidgets import QApplication, QMessageBox, QOpenGLWidget
 2 import sys
 3
 4 try: ❶
 5     from OpenGL import GL
 6 except ImportError:
 7     app = QApplication(sys.argv)
 8     QMessageBox.critical(None, "OpenGL check",
 9             "PyOpenGL must be installed to run this example.")
10     sys.exit(1)
11
12 from OpenGL.GL import * ❷
13 from OpenGL.GLUT import * ❸
14 from OpenGL.GLU import * ❹
15
16 class MainWindow(QOpenGLWidget):
```

```
17      vertex = [
18          [ 0.0, 0.0, 0.0 ],
19          [ 1.0, 0.0, 0.0 ],
20          [ 1.0, 1.0, 0.0 ],
21          [ 0.0, 1.0, 0.0 ],
22          [ 0.0, 0.0, 1.0 ],
23          [ 1.0, 0.0, 1.0 ],
24          [ 1.0, 1.0, 1.0 ],
25          [ 0.0, 1.0, 1.0 ]]
26
27      edge = [
28          [ 0, 1 ],
29          [ 1, 2 ],
30          [ 2, 3 ],
31          [ 3, 0 ],
32          [ 4, 5 ],
33          [ 5, 6 ],
34          [ 6, 7 ],
35          [ 7, 4 ],
36          [ 0, 4 ],
37          [ 1, 5 ],
38          [ 2, 6 ],
39          [ 3, 7 ]]
40
41
42      def __init__(self, parent): 5
43          super(MainWindow, self).__init__(parent)
44          self.setMinimumSize(300, 300)
45
46      def paintGL(self):
47          print("Inside paintGL()")
48          glClearColor(0.0, 0.0, 1.0, 0.0)
49          glClear(GL_COLOR_BUFFER_BIT | GL_DEPTH_BUFFER_BIT)
50          glLoadIdentity()
51
```

```
52
gluLookAt(3.0, 4.0, 5.0, 0.0, 0.0, 0.0, 0.0, 1.0, 0.0)
53
54          glBegin(GL_LINES)
55
56          for i in range(0, 12):
57              glVertex(self.vertex[self.edge[i][0]])
58              glVertex(self.vertex[self.edge[i][1]])
59          glEnd()
60
61          glFlush()
62
63      def resizeGL(self, w, h):
64          print("Inside resizeGL()")
65          glViewport(0, 0, w, h)
66          glMatrixMode(GL_PROJECTION)
67          glLoadIdentity()
68          gluPerspective(30.0, w/h, 1.0, 100.0)
69          glMatrixMode(GL_MODELVIEW)
70
71      def initializeGL(self):
72          print("Inside initializeGL()")
73          glutInitDisplayMode(GLUT_RGBA | GLUT_DOUBLE | GLUT_DEPTH)
74          glClearColor(0.0, 0.0, 0.0, 1.0)
75
76          glClearDepth(1.0)
77          glMatrixMode(GL_PROJECTION)
78          glLoadIdentity()
79          gluPerspective(40.0, 1.0, 1.0, 30.0)
```

1 This try-except block will ensure that PyOpenGL is installed on your system. If not, then the app will exit with an error.

2 3 These modules provide the OpenGL functionality we will need.

4

5. Execute the initialization method of our class. As soon as this executes, control flow switches to *initializeGL()* then *resizeGL()*, then *paintGL()* and back to *initializeGL()* again. Examine the output of the print statements on your terminal to confirm this.

Figure 4.7. Output of the QOpenGLWidget demo on Cygwin

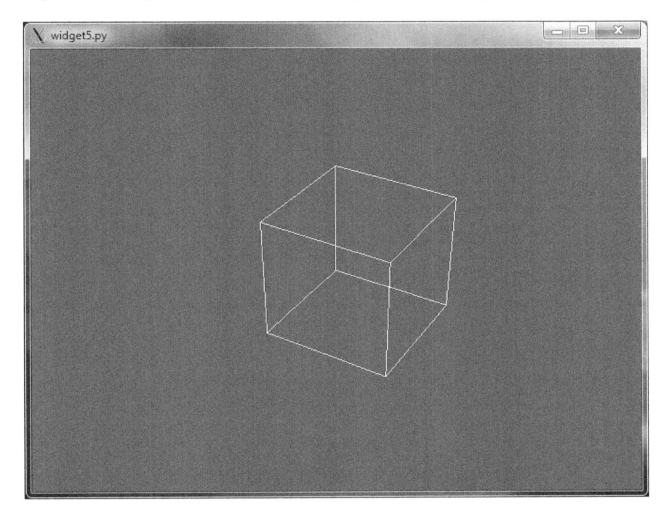

4.7. Miscellaneous widgets

Back when I had fewer cares, I spent a lot of time playing a game called Final Fantasy 7. In my opinion, it has to be one of the best games ever made. Despite its grainy graphics, the story-line and game play are quite captivating. In one of the stages, players are introduced to an imaginary creature called a *Chocobo*.

It looks like a cross between an ostrich and a chicken. Each one of them is unique and, they're all adorable. Players can spend a lot if time at the in-game casino gambling for credits to buy a better chocobo than the one they have. The biggest jackpot occurs when all 3 symbols align at 7, to give you "Lucky 7s". Transliterated into Japanese, "All 7" becomes *Oru 7*.

This subsection will teach you how to make a slot machine simulation using PyQt. Several new widgets are used to make it, so let's get an overview of each of them. The code contained in *widget6.py* simulates our slot machine.

4.7.1. QComboBox

A *QComboBox* provides a means of presenting a list of options to the user in a way that takes up the minimum amount of screen space. The reels of our simulator will be made using this widget. A combobox is a selection widget that displays the current item, and can pop up a list of selectable items. Comboboxes can contain pixmaps as well as strings, in our case we'll use numbers instead of images.

There are two signals emitted if the current item of a combobox changes, *currentIndexChanged()* and *activated()*. *currentIndexChanged()* is always emitted regardless if the change was done programmatically or by user interaction, while *activated()* is only emitted when the change is caused by user interaction. The numerical symbols on our reels will be represented internally as strings. Each time a new combobox item is selected, a signal of type string will be sent to our signal handler.

QComboBox can use the model/view framework to populate its popup list. You can manually specify each of the items in a combobox object using the *addItem()* method, though this tedious and prone to errors when you have a lot of data. In the sim, we use the *setModel()* to specify the model for the combobox. A *QStringListModel* object stores the list of items in our model.

The text of the currently selected item is accessed using the *currentText()* method.

4.7.2. QMovie

The *QMovie* class is a convenience class used to show simple animations without sound. You can instantiate a *QMovie* object by passing in the path to an animated image as its argument. To start the movie, call the *start()* method. QMovie will enter Running state, and emit *started()* and *stateChanged()*. To get the current state of the movie, call *state()*.

4.7.3. QLabel

This widget is used for displaying text or an image. No user interaction functionality is provided. You have already encountered it being used in Chapter 2 to display images. The movie class is overlaid on this widget so it can be displayed.

```python
12 def initUI(self):
13   self.setWindowTitle('Slot machine sim')
14
15   myList = [] ①
16   myList.extend(range(0,10)) ②
17   myList = [str(i) for i in myList] ③
18
19   stringModel = QStringListModel(self) ④
20   stringModel.setStringList(myList) ⑤
21
22   self.comboBox1 = QComboBox(self) ⑥
23 ##         self.comboBox1.addItem("0") ⑦
24 ##         self.comboBox1.addItem("1")
25 ##         self.comboBox1.addItem("2")
26 ##         self.comboBox1.addItem("3")
27 ##         self.comboBox1.addItem("4")
28 ##         self.comboBox1.addItem("5")
29 ##         self.comboBox1.addItem("6")
30 ##         self.comboBox1.addItem("7")
31 ##         self.comboBox1.addItem("8")
32 ##         self.comboBox1.addItem("9")
33   self.comboBox1.setModel(stringModel)
34
35   self.comboBox2 = QComboBox(self)
36   self.comboBox3 = QComboBox(self)
37
38   self.comboBox2.setModel(stringModel)
39   self.comboBox3.setModel(stringModel)
40
41   self.comboBox1.move(50, 50)
42   self.comboBox2.move(100, 50)
43   self.comboBox3.move(150, 50)
44
45   self.movie = QMovie("tenor.gif") ⑧
46
```

```
47    self.label1 = QLabel(self)
48    self.label1.move(50, 100)
49    self.label1.setGeometry(50, 100, 400, 500)
50    self.label1.setMovie(self.movie) 9
51
52    self.comboBox1.activated[str].connect(self.onActivated) 10
53    self.comboBox2.activated[str].connect(self.onActivated) 11
54    self.comboBox3.activated[str].connect(self.onActivated) 12
55
56    self.resize(500, 650)
57    self.show()
58
59 @pyqtSlot(str)
60 def onActivated(self, text):
61   if(self.comboBox1.currentText() == '7' and
self.comboBox2.currentText() == '7'\
62       and self.comboBox3.currentText() == '7'):
63     self.movie.start() 13
64     #self.comboBox1.setEnabled(False)
65     print("Lotto!!!")
```

1 **2** Manually writing out 0 to 9 is tiring. Plus, if your application requires a larger range, you're bound to make a mistake if you manually key in the integers. Python allows us to use the *range()* and *extend()* methods to elegantly populate our list.

3 This uses a list comprehension to convert each element of our list into a string. Our model expects a list containing values of type string.

4 **5** We declare the model that our comboboxes will use. We pass it the list we just created.

6 We declare an instance of our combobox widget.

7 As explained earlier, we can manually create combobox elements as shown here or, we can do it intelligently using a model as shown in lines 33, 38 and 39.

8 We initialize our *QMovie* class and pass it the path to our gif file.

9 We use the *setMovie()* method of *QLabel* to connect the *QMovie* class to a widget.

10 We connect the *activated()* signal from our comboxes to a slot. We pass a string containing

11 the value of the current combobox item.

12

13 If the current value of all three comboboxes is 7, then we play our celebratory movie.

Tip

The *extend()* method appends elements to the end of a list. The resulting list contains all the elements of both lists.

For example:

```
a = [1, 2]
b = [3, "a", "b"]
a.extend(b)
```

When printed out, a contains

```
[1, 2, 3, 'a', 'b']
```

Figure 4.8. Jackpot!

4.8. Summary

This chapter went over the most commonly used widgets in PyQt development.

4.9. References

- https://doc.qt.io/qt-5/qwidget.html#size-prop

- https://doc.qt.io/qt-5/qwidget.html#adjustSize

- https://doc.qt.io/qt-5/QLabel.html#details

- https://doc.qt.io/qt-5/qlineedit.html#textChanged

- https://doc.qt.io/qt-5/qcalendarwidget.html#selectedDate-prop

- https://doc.qt.io/qt-5/qdate.html

- https://doc.qt.io/qt-5/QCheckBox.html#details

- https://doc.qt.io/qt-5/qcheckbox.html#stateChanged

- https://doc.qt.io/qt-5/qt.html#CheckState-enum

- https://doc.qt.io/qt-5/qlcdnumber.html#details

- https://doc.qt.io/qt-5/qslider.html#details

- https://en.wikipedia.org/wiki/FM_broadcast_band

- https://doc.qt.io/qt-5/QProgressBar.html#details

- https://doc.qt.io/qt-5/qtimeline.html#details

- https://doc.qt.io/qt-5/qtimeline.html#frameChanged

- https://doc.qt.io/qt-5/qopenglwidget.html#details

- http://www.not-enough.org/abe/manual/api-aa09/pyqt1.html

- https://codeyarns.com/2018/04/01/how-to-use-cygwin-x-server-for-local-and-remote/

References

- https://forum.qt.io/topic/88035/qxcbconnection-could-not-connt-to-display-cygwin

- https://stackabuse.com/append-vs-extend-in-python-lists/

- https://en.wikipedia.org/wiki/Chocobo

- https://en.wikipedia.org/wiki/Slot_machine

- https://doc.qt.io/qt-5/qcombobox.html

- https://doc.qt.io/qt-5/qstringlistmodel.html

This page intentionally left blank

Chapter 5. FileLister

5.1. Qt Creator

For most large-scale projects you will need to use Qt Creator. This can be downloaded from:
https://www.qt.io/download

The professional version costs about $459 per month(as of July 2018), but the free community version works just as well. Download the community version program appropriate to your operating system. Once you run the setup, a window will appear asking you to create an account on the Qt site. If you don't already have an account with them, do this now.

After you set up Qt Creator, open it.

Figure 5.1. Qt Creator

Go to the File menu and create a new file.

Figure 5.2. New file window

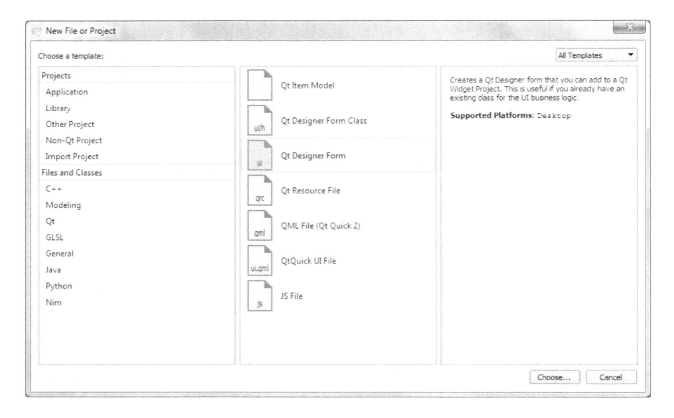

Figure 5.3. Form template selection

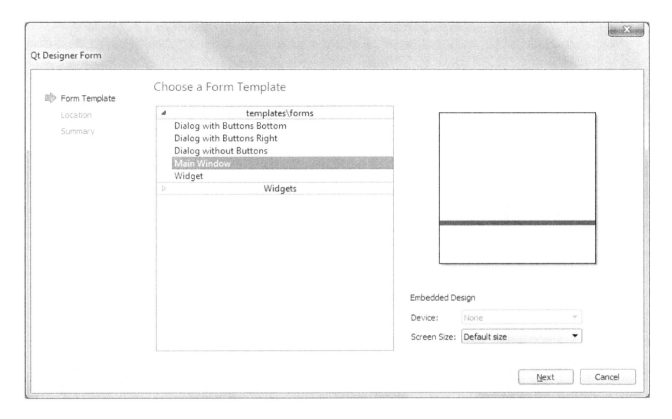

On the next screen, choose "Main Window" as shown.

Save the file in an appropriate location. After that you should get a new form that you can resize, "drag and drop" widgets on etc. Make yourself familiar with the interface, it's pretty simple.

We'll resize our main window a bit, since we don't need it to be that large. We'll also remove the automatically added menu and status bar since we don't plan on using them in this chapter.

All the form elements that your design has as well as their hierarchy, are listed (by default) on the right side of the Qt Creator window under "Object". You can easily remove objects by right clicking on them in that window. For now, we'll just resize our form and delete menu and status bar.

Figure 5.4. Make these adjustments

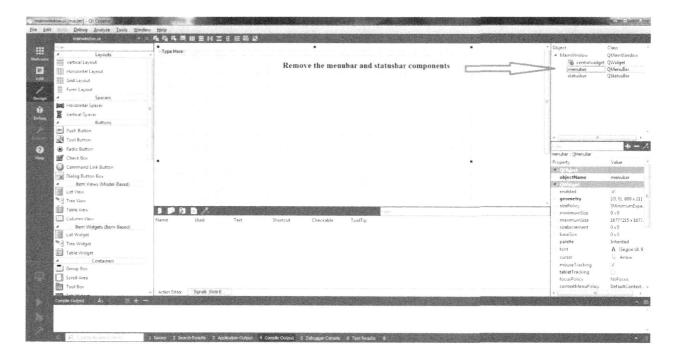

Once we do that, we're left with an (almost) empty form. The only object still left is *centralwidget* but we need it, so we won't change anything about it.

Now drag and drop from the "Widget Box" on the left-hand side a "List Widget" (not List View) widget and a "Push Button", drop them anywhere on the main form.

After resizing the window and its components everything looks perfect, right? Instead of using fixed positions and sizes of the elements in your application you should be using layouts. Fixed positions and sizes will look good on your end (at least until you resize the window) but you can never be sure that they'll look exactly the same on other machines and/or operating systems.

The main window already supports layouts, so we don't need to add any new ones to our form. Simply right click on the "Main Window" under the "Object" inspector and pick "Layout">"Lay out vertically".

Now the windows will scale correctly :)

Figure 5.5. Pick a layout

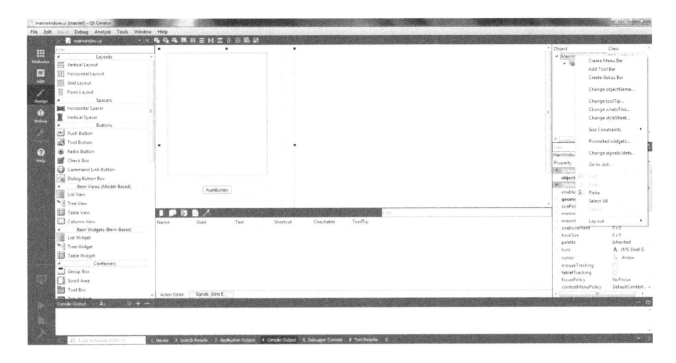

We've nailed the U.I. part down. The only thing left is to give the components meaningful names that we can access in our code. We could stick to the defaults, but to avoid any confusion it's best to rename our components.

Change the button from its default name *pushButton* to *btnBrowse*. Also, change the "text" attribute of the button to *Pick a folder*!

Figure 5.6. Change attributes here

Save the file you've created. In my case, I named the file *mainwindow.ui*

This ".ui" file contains an XML representation of the widgets and properties in their design. For those familiar with Android development, this is like a layout XML file. To convert it into its Python equivalent we use the pyuic5 component. This component was installed along with PyQt5. Once you locate it on your system, run the following command:

pyuic5 mainwindow.ui -o mainwindow.py

You should now have a file called *mainwindow.py*. This is a computer generated file and it's best not to edit it. I will now walk you through the file named *fileLister.py*.

```
1 from PyQt5.QtWidgets import QApplication, QMainWindow, QFileDialog
2 import sys
3 import os
4
5 from mainwindow import Ui_MainWindow  ❶
6
7 class ExampleApp(QMainWindow, Ui_MainWindow):
8     def __init__(self):
9         super(self.__class__, self).__init__()
```

```
10          self.setupUi(self)  # This is defined in the file
automatically generated, mainwindow.py
11                              # It sets up layout and widgets
defined there
12          self.btnBrowse.clicked.connect(self.browse_folder) ❷
13          self.show()
14
15      def browse_folder(self):
16          self.listWidget.clear() # In case there are any
existing elements in the list ❸
17          directory = QFileDialog.getExistingDirectory(self, ❹
18
"Pick a folder")
19          # execute getExistingDirectory dialog and set the
directory variable to be equal
20          # to the user selected directory
21
22          if directory: # if user didn't pick a directory don't
continue ❺
23              for file_name in os.listdir(directory): # for all
files, if any, in the directory ❻
24                  self.listWidget.addItem(file_name)   # add
file to the listWidget ❼
```

❶ We'll also need the file we just generated. Please note that Python is case sensitive! If you change the name from *mainwindow* to *mainWindow*, the interpreter will flag you.

The code is structured as a single class that is derived from the Python object type. The name of the class is the name of the top level object set in Creator with Ui_ prepended. (In the C++ version, the class is defined in the Ui namespace.) We refer to this class as the form class. The class contains a method called *setupUi()*. This takes a single argument which is the widget in which the user interface is created. The type of this argument (typically *QDialog*, *QWidget* or *QMainWindow*) is set in Creator. We refer to this type as the Qt base class. Since the design file will be completely overwritten each time we change something in the design and recreate it, we will not be writing any code in it, instead, we'll create a new class ie *ExampleApp* that we'll combine with the design code so that we can use all of its features.

2 All of the following code is written inside the *ExampleApp* class. Let's start with the *Pick a folder* button. Just like in the previous chapter, we use this line to connect a button event, such as a mouse click, to a function. And add it to the init method of our *ExampleApp* class so that it's set up when the application starts.
self.btnBrowse - btnBrowse is the name of the button object we defined in Qt Creator.

4 To get the directory browser dialog we can use the built in *QtGui.QfileDialog.getExistingDirectory*.

5 If the user picks a directory, the *directory* variable will be equal to the absolute path of the selected directory, otherwise it's set to *None*.

6 This loops through the directory path. For each file found, its name is given to us in the *file_name* variable.

3 7 To add items to the listWidget we use *addItem()* method on it, and to clear all existing items simply use *self.listWidget.clear()*

A file browser dialog will open and the files in the chosen folder will be listed.

Figure 5.7. FileLister output

5.2. Summary

This chapter introduced you to designing apps using Qt Creator. Now it's time to shift gears to something even more complex.

Chapter 6: Currency Exchange Rates App

We will build an app that connects to a web service, gets the exchange rate for some currencies, and then displays that data in a PyQt interface. We will use the currencylayer API(Application programming interface) to do this. Go to:

https://currencylayer.com/signup?plan=1

and sign up for a free account. Then log in, switch to the API tab and retrieve your API key. You will need it soon.

6.1. Designing the UI

If a picture is worth a thousand words, then a video is worth many more. Watch the video at

https://vimeo.com/261681292

The design of the U.I. is shown here. In addition, part 2 shows the linking of the button's click event to the text shown in the labels. Event handling in Qt Creator is done using the Signal/Slot Editor. To assign an event to the button, first click on the button as illustrated in the video. Then hold the F4(or its equivalent if you're on a Mac) button as you drag to the U.I. component you want to be the recipient of the user action. **Review the last minute of the video to see this!**

In the video, clicking the button clears the default text in the *usdLabel* and *audLabel* components. This is done for illustrative purposes, I will override this event handling later on with the response from the currencylayer API.

Convert the U.I. design code from into executable python code with the following command:

pyuic5 -o MainWindow.py -x mainwindow.ui

You already know what the *-o* switch does. The *-x* creates a script you can run right away without any further modification. Run the resulting script and inspect its output:

python MainWindow.py

Figure 6.1. When you click the button, the text on the top 2 labels is cleared

6.2. Switching back to Python

Now we switch back to more familiar territory. The code below is contained in a file named *converter.py*

```
1  from PyQt5 import QtCore, QtGui, QtWidgets
2  from MainWindow import Ui_MainWindow
3
4  class MainWindow(QtWidgets.QMainWindow, Ui_MainWindow):
5      def __init__(self, *args, **kwargs):
6          super(MainWindow, self).__init__(*args, **kwargs)
7          self.setupUi(self)
8
9          self.pushButton.clicked.connect(self.usdLabel.clear)
10         self.pushButton.clicked.connect(self.audLabel.clear)
11         self.pushButton.clicked.connect(self.xauLabel.clear)
12         self.pushButton.clicked.connect(self.btcLabel.clear)
13
14         self.show()
```

```
15
16  if __name__ == "__main__":
17      import sys
18      app = QtWidgets.QApplication(sys.argv)
19      window = MainWindow()
20      sys.exit(app.exec_())
```

When you click the button, the text on all four labels is cleared.

The code to communicate with the web service is covered in the next section.

6.2.1. Web service communication

I've found the python module requests to be one of the easiest socket libraries I've ever used. Even with no past experience, you can get up and running with it in less than five minutes. Let's create a small script that will fetch the latest exchange rates from our web service. Do you have the API key from currencylayer handy? Let's use it here.

I've posted a screenshot of an interactive Python session I had below:

Figure 6.2. Working with the requests module

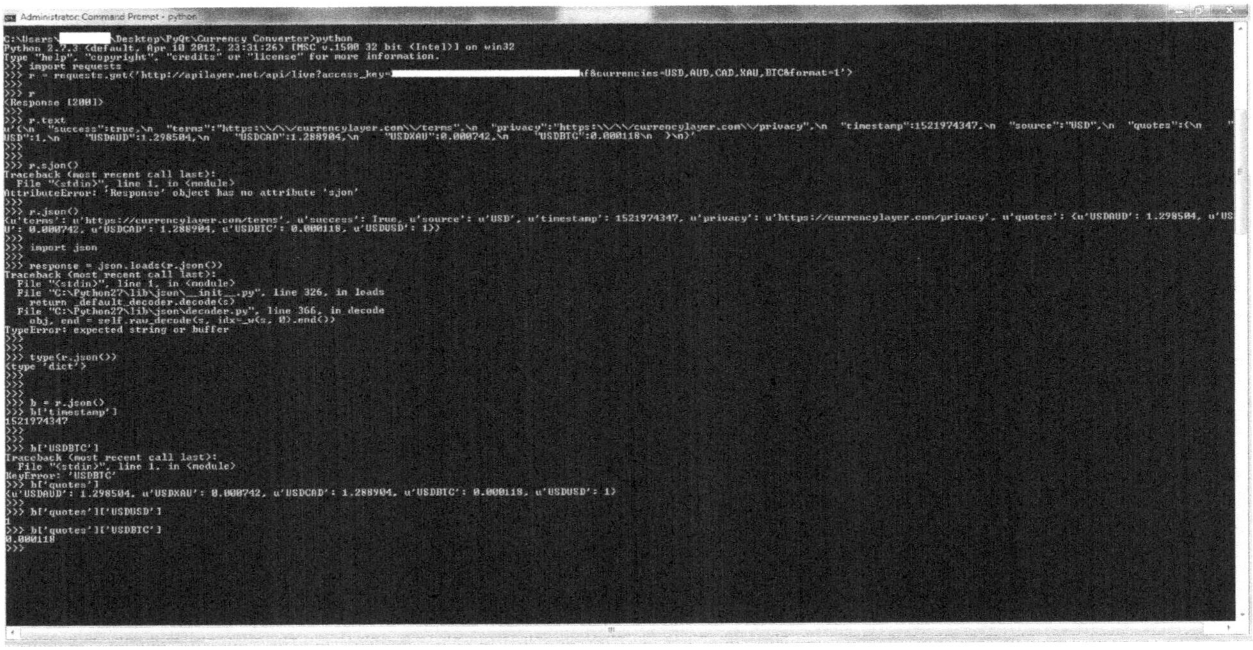

I encourage you to open an interactive session on your computer and try it for yourself. At the very least, open an interactive session and type in the first line:

import requests

If you don't have the requests module installed on your system, you'll get an error message. You can then install the library onto your system. I've created a mock up of my code and saved it as *servicecomm.py*. All you need to do is put in your API key to run it.

```
 1 import requests
 2
 3 CURRENCYLAYER_API_KEY = "put your API key here"
 4
 5 r = requests.get('http://apilayer.net/api/live?access_key='+CURRENCYLAYER_API_KEY+
 6 '&currencies=USD,AUD,CAD,XAU,BTC&format=1') ❶
 7
 8 response = r.json() ❷
 9
10 print(response['quotes']['USDBTC']) ❸
```

❶ A GET request is made to the web service. We pass in as parameters the currencies whose exchange rates we want. The result of our request is stored in a variable named *r*.

❷ The web service response is in JSON(JavaScript Object Notation) format. *r.json()* takes this response and converts it into a Python dict.

❸ We parse our dict and print out the rate for the USDBTC pair.

Tip

A dictionary is a collection which is unordered, changeable and indexed. In Python, dictionaries are written with curly brackets and they have keys and values.

Create and print a dictionary:

```
thisdict = {
  "brand": "Ford",
  "model": "Mustang",
  "year": 1964
}
print(thisdict)
```

Get the value of the "model" key:

```
x = thisdict["model"]
```

If we combine this with the U.I. code from earlier, we'll have a fully functional script.

6.3. Putting it all together

You understand the U.I. code and understand how we communicate with the web service. Now let's put all the code together. The listing for *converterfinal.py* is shown below.

Most of the code should be familiar to you. Just in case you forget to put in an API key, or you're not connected to the internet when you run the script, I've put the code in a try-catch exception block. In case of a system error, exception handling allows you to gracefully continue execution flow without breaking anything.

```
 7  class MainWindow(QtWidgets.QMainWindow, Ui_MainWindow):
 8      def __init__(self, *args, **kwargs):
 9          super(MainWindow, self).__init__(*args, **kwargs)
10          self.setupUi(self)
11
12          self.pushButton.clicked.connect(self.talkToService)
13          self.pushButton.clicked.connect(self.talkToService)
14          self.pushButton.clicked.connect(self.talkToService)
15          self.pushButton.clicked.connect(self.talkToService)
16
17          self.show()
18
19      def talkToService(self):
20          try:
21              r = requests.get('http://apilayer.net/api/live?access_key='+CURRENCYLAYER_API_KEY+
22   '&currencies=USD,AUD,CAD,XAU,BTC&format=1')
23              response = r.json()
24
```

Chapter 6: Currency Exchange Rates App

```
25            self.usdLabel.setText(str(response['quotes']
['USDUSD']))  ❶
26            self.audLabel.setText(str(response['quotes']
['USDAUD']))  ❷
27            self.xauLabel.setText(str(response['quotes']
['USDXAU']))  ❸
28            self.btcLabel.setText(str(response['quotes']
['USDBTC']))  ❹
29        except:
30            QtWidgets.QMessageBox.critical(self, "Exception",  ❺
31                                           "Something went wrong!")
```

❺ In an ideal situation only the code in the try block(lines 21-28) runs. In case anything goes wrong for example: no Internet connection, no API key, or anything else unforeseen, the except block(line30) is called.

❶ ❷ ❸ ❹ These lines depend on recieving valid output from our call to the web service. If it doesn't get this, then the variables will be empty. Printing non-existent variables will cause the script to break.

The *setText* method of the *QLabel* component allows us to set the text of our labels.

Have a look at the code on line 25 inside the brackets.

str(response['quotes']['USDUSD'])

This illustrates type-casting. The *setText* method expects a variable of type string, yet *response['quotes']['USDUSD']* returns a floating point real number. To convert a real number into a string we wrap it inside a *str()* function.

6.4. Summary

This chapter showed you how to add internet functionality to your apps. If you understand the interaction your target(e.g. a web service) expects, you can quickly set up a demo or a working app for your clients quite rapidly.

6.5. References

- https://doc.qt.io/qt-5/qmessagebox.html

- https://doc.qt.io/qt-5/qlabel.html#text-prop

- https://docs.python.org/3/tutorial/errors.html

- http://docs.python-requests.org/en/master/user/quickstart/

- https://doc.qt.io/qt-5/qlabel.html

- https://www.w3schools.com/python/python_dictionaries.asp

This page intentionally left blank

Chapter 7: PyQt databases and CSS styling

So far we've used the QT widgets just as they were shipped from the Qt Company. However, it's possible to customize their look and feel. But, before we begin we'll cover the basics of databases.

7.1. Qt Databases

I assume you have a basic understanding of relational databases and SQL commands. PyQt5 is capable of interfacing with several types of databases including: MySQL, PostgreSQL, SQLite and ODBC. For the sake of uniformity across different platforms, we will work with SQLite in this chapter. For those who don't have a preferred SQLite browser, check out:

https://sqlitebrowser.org/

The database we will use is in this chapter's folder and is called *pyqt101.db*.

7.1.1. Connecting to the database and querying it

The code below is contained in a file named *connection-test.py*.

```
 1  from PyQt5.QtWidgets import QMessageBox, QApplication
 2  from PyQt5.QtSql import QSqlDatabase, QSqlQuery
 3
 4  def createConnection():
 5      filename = os.path.join(os.path.dirname(__file__), "pyqt101.db")
 6
 7      db = QSqlDatabase.addDatabase('QSQLITE')  ❶
 8      db.setDatabaseName(filename)  ❷
 9
10      if not db.open():  ❸
11          QMessageBox.critical(None, "Cannot open database",  ❹
12              "Unable to establish a database connection.\n",
```

```
13                    QMessageBox.Cancel)
14        return False  [5]
15
16    query = QSqlQuery()
17
18    result = query.exec_("SELECT Name FROM `authors`")  [6]
19
20    while query.next():
21        print(query.value(0))  [7]
22        #print(query.value("Name"))
23
24    db.close()  [8]
25
26 if __name__ == '__main__':
27
28     import sys
29     import os
30     app = QApplication(sys.argv)
31     createConnection()
```

[1] The QsqlDatabase class handles a connection to a database. An instance of QSqlDatabase represents the connection. The connection provides access to the database via one of the supported database drivers, which are derived from QSqlDriver. Create a connection by calling one of the static *addDatabase()* functions, where you specify the driver or type of driver to use (depending on the type of database) and a connection name.

[2] Once the QSqlDatabase object has been created, set the connection parameters with *setDatabaseName()*, *setUserName()*, *setPassword()*, *setHostName()*, *setPort()*, and *setConnectOptions()*. Then call *open()* to activate the physical connection to the database. The connection is not usable until you open it. Some of the connection parameters listed are optional. We only specify the database name parameter in this instance.

[3] [4] We must anticipate problems while opening the database and allow our script to exit gracefully.

[5]

[6] The QSqlQuery class provides a means of executing and manipulating SQL statements. This class can be used to execute DML(data manipulation language) statements, such as SELECT, INSERT, UPDATE and DELETE, as well as DDL(data definition language) statements, such as CREATE TABLE. Successfully executed SQL statements set the query's state to active so

that *isActive()* returns true. Otherwise, the query's state is set to inactive. You can loop through your results by checking whether the active state is true or not. Most times you can use the

exec(<put your SQL query here>)

method to execute your queries as shown in line 18 of the code. It returns true if the query was successful. Otherwise, if you need to use parameters in your queries use the

prepare(<put your SQL query here>)

method.

7 Navigating records is performed with the following functions:

- *next()*

- *previous()*

- *first()*

- *last()*

- *seek()*

These functions allow you to move forward, backward or arbitrarily through the records returned by the query. If you only need to move forward through the results (e.g., by using *next()*), you can use *setForwardOnly()*, which will save a significant amount of memory overhead and improve performance on some databases. Once an active query is positioned on a valid record, data can be retrieved using *value()* as shown in line 21 of the code.

The *value()* function can take a numerical index or a string as a parameter, although the string variant is considered less efficient.

8 It's always a good habit to *close()* your database connection and free any acquired resources.

7.2. Models

Often the data from a database is displayed using PyQt components like lists or tables. PyQt provides two classes that extract data directly from the database:

1. QsqlQueryModel

2. QSqlTableModel

We examine QsqlQueryModel first, since it's easier to understand.

7.2.1. QsqlQueryModel

The QSqlQueryModel class provides a read-only data model for SQL result sets. You can read database entries, but you can't create, update or delete them. This class has a number of functions all of which can be looked up at:

https://doc.qt.io/Qt-5/qsqlquerymodel.html

We'll cover the more pertinent ones which are used in *model0.py*. An excerpt from this file is shown below.

```
19  if not db.open():
20      QMessageBox.critical(None, "Cannot open database",
21          "Unable to establish a database connection.\n",
22          QMessageBox.Cancel)
23      return False
24
25  sqm = QSqlQueryModel(parent = self)
26  sqm.setQuery("SELECT * FROM `authors`")   [1]
27
28  sqm.setHeaderData(1, Qt.Horizontal, 'Author names')   [2]
29
30  self.setModel(sqm)   [3]
31  self.hideColumn(0)   [4]
32  db.close()
```

[1] *setQuery(<sql query here>, <optional parameter to specify database to be queried>)*

This is where you input your SQL query. If no database is specified, then the default connection will be used.

[2] *setHeaderData(<int index>, <Qt::Orientation orientation i.e. Horizontal or Vertical>, <string value>, <role>)*

Have a look at line 25! Our class is an instance of QTableView, so what we do in line 28 will be shown in a table. The *index* parameter specifies the index of the value we want to display from our query results. *Orientation* specifies whether our header will be horizontal or vertical. *Value* specifies the header name.

3 QTableView implements a table view that displays items from a model. We specify the model it should use to display its data on line 30. By default, all the data contained in the authors table, that is the author name and author id will be displayed.

4 Line 31 hides the author id column, so only author names are displayed.

Model–view–controller is an architectural pattern commonly used for developing user interfaces that divides an application into three interconnected parts. This is done to separate internal representations of information from the way information is presented to and accepted from the user. The MVC design pattern decouples these major components allowing for efficient code reuse and parallel development.

Figure 7.1. Image courtesy of qt.io

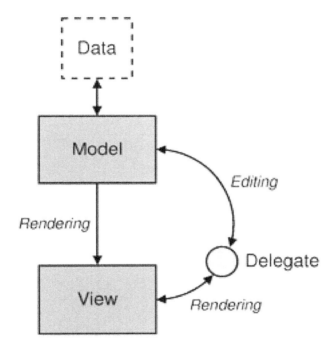

If the view and the controller objects are combined, the result is the model/view architecture. This still separates the way that data is stored from the way that it is presented to the user, but provides a simpler framework based on the same principles. This separation makes it possible to display the same data in several views, and to implement new types of views, without changing the underlying data structures. To allow flexible handling of user input, we introduce the concept of the delegate. The advantage of having a delegate in this framework is that it allows the way items of data are rendered and edited to be customized.

Those who would like to further acquaint themselves with MVC can look up the following resources:

https://doc.qt.io/qt-5/model-view-programming.html

https://en.wikipedia.org/wiki/Model%E2%80%93view%E2%80%93controller

7.2.2. QsqlTableModel

It's fun navigating through databases in read-only mode, but it quickly becomes boring. In order to perform CRUD(Create, Read, Update, Delete) operations on a database you need to use the QsqlTableModel class. This class provides an editable data model for a single database table. An exhaustive list of its functions can be found at:

https://doc.qt.io/qt-5/qsqltablemodel.html

I will explain the most common ones using an example script. The code for the listing below can be found in *model2.py* in this chapter's folder. I attempted to create a pure Model-View example, but felt that it wasn't good enough. Open *model1.py* to see my attempt.

```
1  from PyQt5.QtWidgets import QMessageBox, QApplication, QTableView, QVBoxLayout, QPushButton, QWidget
2  from PyQt5.QtSql import QSqlDatabase, QSqlTableModel
3  from PyQt5.QtCore import Qt
4
5  def initializeModel(model):
6      model.setTable('authors1')  ❶
7      model.setEditStrategy(QSqlTableModel.OnFieldChange)  ❷
8      model.select()  ❸
9      model.setHeaderData(1, Qt.Horizontal, 'Author name(s)')
10
11 def createView(model):
12     view = QTableView()
13     view.setModel(model)
14     view.resize(230, 254)
15     view.hideColumn(0)
16     view.setColumnWidth(1, 200)
17     return view
18
19 def addRecord():
20     # We insert an empty record into which the user can enter their data
```

```
21      sqm.insertRow(sqm.rowCount())  ❹
22
23  def delRecord() :
24      sqm.removeRow(view1.currentIndex().row())  ❺
25      # We reload the data in the model, to remove an empty
"garbage" record
26      sqm.select()  ❻
```

❶ I created an extra copy of the authors table for you to experiment with. I want to preserve the relationships between the original tables for the next section.

❷ We pass an enumerated type to the edit strategy function on line 7. Other possible values and their meanings are shown below.

Constant	Value	Description
QsqlTableModel.OnFieldChange	0	All changes to the model will be applied immediately to the database.
QsqlTableModel.OnRowChange	1	Changes to a row will be applied when the user selects a different row.
QsqlTableModel.OnManualSubmit	2	All changes will be cached in the model until either submitAll() or revertAll() is called.

As soon as we make any changes to any row in our table, the values are immediately written to the database. In more complex systems you may want to store all your changes in a cache, then write them all at once. But for simple scripts like this, I've chosen to write all row changes as soon as they're made.

❸ ❻ The *select()* function in lines 8 and 26 refreshes the data in the model. On line 26, after deleting a selected row, the model is reloaded to remove the empty row in the database. In an ideal situation, you should be able to completely separate the user interface and data management code. But, the interaction between *delRecord()* and the U.I. breaks this flow.

❺ *view1.currentIndex()* on line 24 returns the model index of the current item. The *row()* appended to it returns the model this index refers to. When you first run this script as shown in Figure 7.2, the model index automatically points at the first row in our table view. When you click the delete button, the first row is automatically deleted. But if you subsequently click on delete without highlighting a row, nothing will be deleted.

4 If the database supports returning the size of a query, the number of rows of the current query is returned. Otherwise, *rowCount()* on line 21 returns the number of rows currently cached on the client.

```
insertRow(<position x>)
```

adds a row at the x+1 row of the model.

Go ahead and run *model2.py*. To insert a new record, click the appropriate button. A new row will be added after the last row of the table. Double click on this row to edit it and press the Enter key on your keyboard after you've finished. To delete a row, first highlight it with your mouse and click on the delete button.

Figure 7.2. QsqlTableModel demo

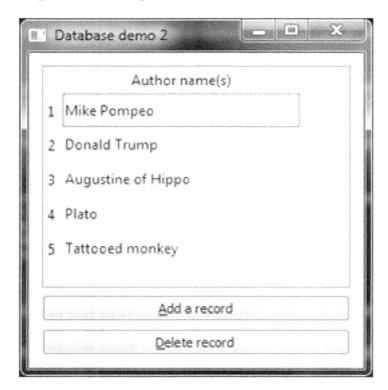

7.2.3. QsqlRelationalTableModel

All our work with databases so far has involved working with a single table. But the real power of databases comes from aggregating various tables together and presenting an interface to manipulate these components as one.

The QSqlRelationalTableModel class inherits all its methods from the QSqlTableMode1 class and, in addition to them, defines the following methods that you may find useful:

1. *setRelation(<specify column index>, <QsqlRelation relation>)*: Lets the specified *column* be a foreign index specified by *relation*.

2. *setJoinMode(<Binding mode>)*: Specifies the binding mode for the entire model. We pass an enumerated type here. Its possible values and their meanings are shown below:

Constant	Value	Description
QSqlRelationalTableModel.InnerJoin	0	Inner join mode, return rows when there is at least one match in both tables.
QSqlRelationalTableModel.LeftJoin	1	Left join mode, returns all rows from the left table (table_name1), even if there are no matches in the right table (table_name2).

Figure 7.3. Lines 9 and 10 commented out

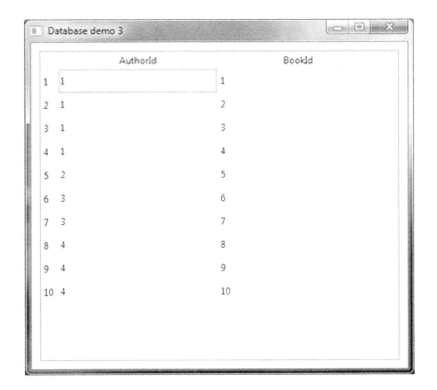

Chapter 7: PyQt databases and
CSS styling

Figure 7.4. Line 10 commented out

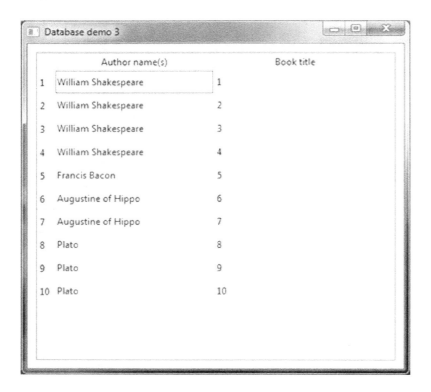

Figure 7.5. Lines 9 and 10 both included

Let's examine the code for *model3.py*. I've mostly recycled the code for model2.py, and I'll explain the changes I've made in it.

```
 1 from PyQt5.QtWidgets import QMessageBox, QApplication, QTableView, QVBoxLayout, QPushButton, QWidget
 2 from PyQt5.QtSql import QSqlDatabase, QSqlRelationalTableModel, QSqlRelation, QSqlRelationalDelegate, QSqlTableModel
 3 from PyQt5.QtCore import Qt
 4
 5 def initializeModel(model):
 6     model.setTable('booksauthors')
 7     model.setEditStrategy(QSqlTableModel.OnManualSubmit)
 8     model.dataChanged.connect(model.submitAll)
 9     model.setRelation(0, QSqlRelation("authors", "id", "name")) ❶
10     model.setRelation(1, QSqlRelation("books", "id", "title"))❷
11     model.setHeaderData(0, Qt.Horizontal, 'Author name(s)')
12     model.setHeaderData(1, Qt.Horizontal, 'Book title')
13     model.select()
```

❶ The table view uses the model from the *booksauthors* table. If you run it now with both lines 9 and 10 commented out you get output similar to that shown in Figure 7.3. This simply reads the table and outputs its contents.

When the interpreter encounters

"authors", "id", "name"

on line 7, it takes the first column shown in Figure 7.3, then for every integer value x it goes into the *authors* table and looks up the row whose *authorid* has a value of x. Then, from that row, it returns the corresponding value of the *name* column. For example, the first row in the *booksauthors* table has an *authorid* value of 1. PyQt takes this value of 1 and looks into the *authors* table to find the row whose *id* column also has a value of 1. Then from that row, it reads the value of the name column, which in this case is *William Shakespeare*.

❷ This line does something similar for the books table to give you what you see in Figure 7.5.

7.2.4. QSqlRelationalDelegate

I commented out the buttons in the previous example, because changes you make to the model aren't saved to the database. The QSqlRelationalDelegate class provides a delegate that is used to display and edit data from a QsqlRelationalTableModel. It provides a combobox for fields that are foreign keys into other tables.

Figure 7.6. Using the QSqlRelationalDelegate class

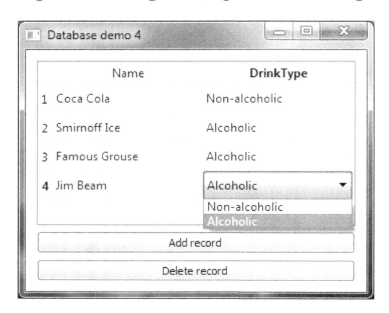

For the sake of pedagogy, we will use a simpler data model than before. In *pyqt101.db* there are two tables: *drinks* and *category*. Drinks contains a list of well-known drinks, like Fanta, Johnny Walker etc. We classify these into two different categories: alcoholic or non-alcoholic. The categories table contains these 2 categories. Have a look at *model4.py*. Most of it should be familiar to you based on what we've previously covered.

```
1 from PyQt5.QtWidgets import QMessageBox, QApplication, QTableView, QVBoxLayout, QPushButton, QWidget
2 from PyQt5.QtSql import QSqlDatabase, QSqlRelationalTableModel, QSqlTableModel, QSqlRelation, QSqlRelationalDelegate
3 from PyQt5.QtCore import Qt
4
5 def initializeModel(model):
6     model.setTable('drinks')
```

```
 7        model.setEditStrategy(QSqlTableModel.OnRowChange) ❶
 8        model.setHeaderData(1, Qt.Horizontal, 'Name')
 9        model.setHeaderData(2, Qt.Horizontal, 'Type of drink')
10        model.setRelation(2,
QSqlRelation('category', 'id', 'drinktype'))
11        model.select()
12
13 def createView(model):
14        view = QTableView()
15        view.setModel(model)
16        view.setItemDelegate(QSqlRelationalDelegate(view)) ❷
17        view.hideColumn(0)
18        view.setColumnWidth(1, 150)
19        view.setColumnWidth(2, 150)
20        return view
21
22 def addRecord():
23        model.insertRow(model.rowCount())
24        view.scrollToBottom() ❸
25
26 def delRecord():
27        model.deleteRowFromTable(view.currentIndex().row()) ❹
28        model.select()
```

❶ The first difference is on this line. We write to our database any time that changes to a row in our model are made.

❷ Unlike our previous example, we set the item delegate for the whole view as shown here.

❸ This line automatically scrolls down to the last row of our view.

❹ The most drastic departure from our previous script is on this line. Earlier on we'd used the *removeRow()* method. However, when used here, changes are only made to the model and aren't written to the database. If we want to commit our changes to the database, we must use *deleteRowFromTable()*.

Have you run the script yet? The view is a bit quirky. When you add a new row, be sure to press Enter on your keyboard after you enter in all the required data. When the asterisk in the leftmost column changes and becomes a number, then you can rest assured that the data has been written to the database.

7.3. CSS Styling

Style sheets in Qt5 are based on the CSS2 specification which can be found at:

https://www.w3.org/TR/2011/REC-CSS2-20110607/#minitoc

We will cover the basic rules and then look at a pretty cool example.

7.3.1. Style Rules

In the style rule below, *QPushButton* is the selector and *{ color: red }* is the declaration. The rule specifies that QPushButton and its subclasses should use red as their foreground text color.

Qt Style Sheet is generally case insensitive (i.e., *color, Color, COLOR,* and *cOloR* refer to the same property). The only exceptions are class names, object names, and Qt property names, which are case sensitive.

Several selectors can be specified for the same declaration, using commas (,) to separate the selectors. For example, the rule

```
QPushButton, QLineEdit, QComboBox { color: red }
```

is equivalent to this sequence of three rules:

```
QPushButton { color: red }
QLineEdit { color: red }
QComboBox { color: red }
```

The declaration part of a style rule is a list of property: value pairs, enclosed in braces and separated with semicolons. For example:

```
QPushButton { color: red; background-color: white }
```

A list of properties that you can manipulate can be found at:

https://doc.qt.io/Qt-5/stylesheet-reference.html#list-of-properties

7.3.2. Selector Types

All the examples so far have used the simplest type of selector- the Type Selector. Qt Style Sheets support all the selectors defined in CSS2. The table below summarizes the most useful types of selectors.

Selector	Example	Explanation
Universal Selector	*	Matches all widgets.
Type Selector	QPushButton	Matches instances of QPushButton and of its subclasses.
Property Selector	QPushButton[flat="false"]	Matches instances of QPushButton that are not flat. This selector may also be used to test dynamic properties. Instead of =, you can also use ~= to test whether a Qt property of type QStringList contains a given QString.
Class Selector	.QPushButton	Matches instances of QPushButton, but not of its subclasses. This is equivalent to *[class~="QPushButton"].
ID Selector	QPushButton#okButton	Matches all QPushButton instances whose object name is okButton.
Descendant Selector	QDialog QPushButton	Matches all instances of QPushButton that are descendants (children, grandchildren, etc.) of a QDialog.
Child Selector	QDialog > QPushButton	Matches all instances of QPushButton that are direct children of a QDialog.

7.3.3. Sub-Controls

For styling complex widgets, it is necessary to access subcontrols of the widget, such as the drop-down button of a QComboBox or the up and down arrows of a QSpinBox. Selectors may contain subcontrols that make it possible to restrict the application of a rule to specific widget subcontrols. For example:

`QComboBox::drop-down { image: url(dropdown.png) }`

The above rule styles the drop-down button of all QComboBoxes. Sub-controls are always positioned with respect to another element – a reference element. This reference element could be the widget or another Sub-control. For example, the *::drop-down* of a QComboBox is placed, by default, in the top right corner of the Padding rectangle of the QcomboBox.

A list of Stylable Widgets for the Sub-controls to use to style a widget and their default positions can be found at:

https://doc.qt.io/Qt-5/stylesheet-reference.html#list-of-stylable-widgets

A list of supported sub-controls can be found at:

https://doc.qt.io/Qt-5/stylesheet-reference.html#list-of-sub-controls

7.3.4. Pseudo-States

Selectors may contain pseudo-states that restrict the application of the rule based on the widget's state. Pseudo-states appear at the end of the selector, with a colon (:) in between. For example, the following rule applies when the mouse hovers over a QPushButton:

`QPushButton:hover { color: white }`

Pseudo-states can be negated using the exclamation operator. For example, the following rule applies when the mouse does not hover over a QRadioButton:

`QRadioButton:!hover { color: red }`

Pseudo-states can be chained, in which case a logical AND is implied. For example, the following rule applies to when the mouse hovers over a checked QCheckBox:

`QCheckBox:hover:checked { color: white }`

Negated Pseudo-states may appear in Pseudo-state chains. For example, the following rule applies when the mouse hovers over a QPushButton that is not pressed:

`QPushButton:hover:!pressed { color: blue; }`

If needed, logical OR can be expressed using the comma operator:

```
QCheckBox:hover, QCheckBox:checked { color: white }
```

Pseudo-states can appear in combination with subcontrols. For example:

```
QComboBox::drop-down:hover { image: url(dropdown_bright.png) }
```

A complete list of pseudo-states provided by Qt widgets can be found at:
https://doc.qt.io/Qt-5/stylesheet-reference.html#list-of-pseudo-states

7.3.5. Conflict Resolution

Conflicts arise when several style rules specify the same properties with different values. Consider the following:

```
QPushButton#okButton { color: gray }
QPushButton { color: red }
```

Both rules match QPushButton instances called okButton and there is a conflict for the color property. To resolve this conflict, we must take into account the **specificity** of the selectors. In the above example, QPushButton#okButton is considered more specific than QPushButton, because it (usually) refers to a single object, not to all instances of a class.

Similarly, selectors with pseudo-states are more specific than ones that do not specify pseudo-states. Thus, the following style specifies that a QPushButton should have white text when the mouse is hovering over it, otherwise red text:

```
QPushButton:hover { color: white }
QPushButton { color: red }
```

Here's a tricky one:

```
QPushButton:hover { color: white }
QPushButton:enabled { color: red }
```

Here, both selectors have the same specificity, so if the mouse hovers over the button while it is enabled, the second rule takes precedence. If we want the text to be white in that case, we can reorder the rules like this:

```
QPushButton:enabled { color: red }
QPushButton:hover { color: white }
```

Alternatively, we can make the first rule more specific:

```
QPushButton:hover:enabled { color: white }
QPushButton:enabled { color: red }
```

For determining the specificity of a rule, Qt Style Sheets follow the CSS2 Specification which can be found at:

http://www.w3.org/TR/REC-CSS2/cascade.html#specificity

7.3.6. Cascading

Style sheets can be set on the QApplication, on parent widgets, and on child widgets. An arbitrary widget's effective style sheet is obtained by merging the style sheets set on the widget's ancestors (parent, grandparent, etc.), as well as any style sheet set on the QApplication.

When conflicts arise, the widget's own style sheet is always preferred to any inherited style sheet, irrespective of the specificity of the conflicting rules. Likewise, the parent widget's style sheet is preferred to the grandparent's, etc.

One consequence of this is that setting a style rule on a widget automatically gives it precedence over other rules specified in the ancestor widgets' style sheets or the QApplication style sheet. Consider the following example. First, we set a style sheet on the QApplication:

```
qApp->setStyleSheet("QPushButton { color: white }");
```

Then we set a style sheet on a QPushButton object:

```
myPushButton->setStyleSheet("* { color: blue }");
```

The style sheet on the QPushButton forces the QPushButton (and any child widget) to have blue text, in spite of the more specific rule set provided by the application-wide style sheet.

7.3.7. Inheritance

In classic CSS, when font and color of an item is not explicitly set, it gets automatically inherited from the parent. By default, when using Qt Style Sheets, a widget does **not** automatically inherit its font and color setting from its parent widget.

For example, consider a QPushButton inside a QGroupBox:

```
qApp->setStyleSheet("QGroupBox { color: red; } ");
```

The QPushButton does not have an explicit color set. Hence, instead of inheriting color of its parent QGroupBox, it has the system color. If we want to set the color on a QGroupBox and its children, we can write:

```
qApp->setStyleSheet("QGroupBox, QGroupBox * { color: red; }");
```

In contrast, setting a font and palette using QWidget::setFont() and QWidget::setPalette() propagates to child widgets.

If you would prefer that the font and palette propagate to child widgets, you can set the *Qt.AA_UseStyleSheetPropagationInWidgetStyles* flag, like this:

```
QCoreApplication.setAttribute(Qt. \
 AA_UseStyleSheetPropagationInWidgetStyles, True)
```

When the widget-style font and palette propagation is enabled, font and palette changes made through Qt Style Sheets will behave as though the user had manually called the corresponding *QWidget.setPalette()* and *QWidget.setFont()* methods on all of the QWidgets targeted by the style sheet.

To help you understand this better have a look at *cssinheritance.py*.

```
58  if __name__ == '__main__':
59      app = QApplication(sys.argv)
60
61      app.setStyleSheet("QGroupBox { color: red; } ")
62
63      #app.setStyleSheet("QGroupBox, QGroupBox * { color: red; }")
64
65      #QCoreApplication.setAttribute(Qt. \
66    AA_UseStyleSheetPropagationInWidgetStyles, True)
67      #app.setStyleSheet("QGroupBox { color: red; } ")
68
69      clock = Window()
70      clock.show()
71      sys.exit(app.exec_())
```

Chapter 7: PyQt databases and CSS styling 86

First, run it as it is to see the default. Comment out line 61 and un-comment line 63 to see the effect of "brute-forcing" inheritance. This may have unforeseen consequences somewhere down the line. Comment out lines 61 and 63 and un-comment lines 65 and 66 to see the more elegant way of setting up inheritance.

Have a look at line 61 again! It illustrates one way to set styling one widget at a time, by calling the *setStyleSheet()* method on all your widgets. I will demonstrate how to set global CSS properties in the next section.

7.3.8. Example

Now for the demo that inspired me to write this section on CSS. Drum-roll… I found this code online on a website called "ilycode". At the time of publishing, the blog I found this article on was password-protected. I'll leave a link to the blog article in the references section.

Figure 7.7. Before applying CSS

In the chapter folder, run the script called *css-pre.py* to get something similar to what is shown above. The script presents the U.I. for a simple client registration page. Given what you already know about databases, you can create a back-end to process the registration details. Apart from lines 23-27, all the code in this script should be familiar to you. These lines set up a label. However, instead of putting text in the label, we load an image.

Run the script called *css-post.py* to see the effect of applying CSS styling to the UI.

Figure 7.8. After applying CSS

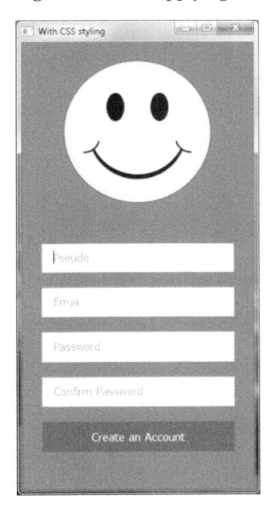

This script sets CSS properties on widget-by-widget basis. This is usually disadvantageous because you have to keep repeating things. For example the text widgets on lines 33, 39, 45, 51, all repeat the following code:

```
setStyleSheet("background-color:#f7f7f7; color:#8e8e8e; padding-top: 5px; font-size:15px; padding-left:10px")
```

Chapter 7: PyQt databases and
CSS styling

Apart from setting styling code locally, you can also set it up globally. Have a look at the code in *css-post-global.py*.

A variable is declared on line 11 that contains all the Style Sheet attributes for the script in one place. This Style Sheet is then applied on the QApplication instance as shown in line 37. If you want to override the style attributes for any widget, you can specify a widget-specific Style Sheet as shown on line 57.

```
 5  class MainWindow:
 6      def __init__(self):
 7          self.app = QtWidgets.QApplication(sys.argv)
 8          self.window = QtWidgets.QMainWindow()
 9          self.imagePath = "240px-Smiley.svg.png"
10
11          self.stylesheet = """
12
13          QPushButton{
14              background-color:#4e4e4e;
15              color:#ffffff;
16              font-size:15px;
17              border:1px solid #4e4e4e;
18          }
19
20          QMainWindow{
21              background-color:#ff9900;
22              /*background-color:#6e6e6e;*/
23          }
24
25          QTextEdit{
26              background-color:#44ff22;
27          }
28
29
30          """
31
32          self.initGUI()
```

```
33
34          self.window.setWindowTitle("With CSS styling")
35          self.window.setGeometry(500, 100, 300,600)
36          self.window.show()
37          self.app.setStyleSheet(self.stylesheet)
38          sys.exit(self.app.exec_())
39
40      def initGUI(self):
41
42          #create a label
43          self.image = QtGui.QImage(self.imagePath)
44          self.label = QtWidgets.QLabel(self.window)
45          self.label.setGeometry(50,20, 200,200)
46
self.label.setPixmap(QtGui.QPixmap.fromImage(self.image))
47          self.label.setScaledContents(True)
48
49          #create a pseudo field
50          self.pseudo = QtWidgets.QTextEdit(self.window)
51          self.pseudo.setGeometry(25,270,250,40)
52          self.pseudo.setText("Pseudo")
53
54          #create an email field
55          self.email = QtWidgets.QTextEdit(self.window)
56          self.email.setGeometry(25, 330,250,40)
57          self.email.setStyleSheet("background-color:#f7f7f7;
color:#8e8e8e; padding-top: 5px; font-size:15px; padding-
left:10px")
58          self.email.setText("Email")
59
60          #create a password field
61          self.password = QtWidgets.QTextEdit(self.window)
```

It's amazing how a few lines of code can dramatically enhance your app. The illustration below shows our app with line 61 of *css-post-global.py* commented out.

Figure 7.9. Eye candy

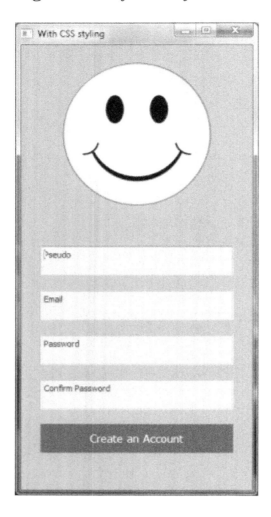

7.4. Summary

Many complex apps use databases to store some of their data. This chapter has introduced you to using databases in your apps. Although we've worked with SQLite databases, it's important to keep in mind that the same techniques will apply to MySQL or any other database supported by the PyQt framework.

CSS can help you soup up your U.I. Use it whenever you can to draw your client's attention to specific parts of your interface and to make your apps look attractive.

7.5. References

- https://doc.qt.io/qt-5/qsqldatabase.html

- https://doc.qt.io/qt-5/qsqlquery.html

- https://doc.qt.io/qt-5.11/qsqldatabase.html

- https://doc.qt.io/Qt-5/qsqlquerymodel.html

- https://doc.qt.io/qt-5/qtableview.html

- https://doc.qt.io/qt-5/qsqltablemodel.html#EditStrategy-enum

- https://doc.qt.io/qt-5/qtsql-tablemodel-example.html

- https://doc.qt.io/qt-5/qabstractitemview.html#currentIndex

- https://doc.qt.io/qt-5/qmodelindex.html#row

- https://doc.qt.io/qt-5/qsqlrelationaltablemodel.html

- https://doc.qt.io/qt-5/qsqlrelationaldelegate.html

- https://doc.qt.io/qt-5/qsqlrelationaltablemodel.html#JoinMode-enum

- https://doc.qt.io/Qt-5/stylesheet-syntax.html

- https://doc.qt.io/qt-5/stylesheet-reference.html

- https://ilycode.com/index.php/gui-application-using-python-and-pyqt5/pyqt5-5-cascading-style-sheets-in-pyqt5/

- https://www.w3.org/TR/2011/REC-CSS2-20110607/#minitoc

- https://doc.qt.io/Qt-5/stylesheet-examples.html

- https://pythonprogramminglanguage.com/pyqt5-groupbox/

Chapter 8: Radio App

In this chapter we'll explore a radio app that uses PyQt5. I spent about 2 days struggling to set up the environment for this on my Windows system, before I finally gave up and switched to Linux. I highly recommend you follow along on a Unix-like system.

Important

For Windows users, you may refer to Appendix C for instructions on how to set up cygwin, so that you may follow along.

For Windows users, you don't need to create a separate partition and install Linux. You can set up an Ubuntu system on a virtual machine. For those following along on Unix-like systems other than Ubuntu, I trust that you'll be able to adapt the install instructions to suit your particular OS.

8.1. Setting up

You first need to set up a Python module called *gi*. This is usually found in the PyGObject package. To install this on Ubuntu switch to your CLI and run the following:

sudo apt-get install python-gi python-gi-cairo python3-gi python3-gi-cairo gir1.2-gtk-3.0

This will install the gi module on your system if you didn't already have it. To ensure that it works, run the script titled *hello.py* in the source folder for this chapter. For users who've just switched from Windows, you have to explicitly invoke python3 since your system will probably also have python2.

If everything goes well your output should look similar to the following:

Figure 8.1. Is *gi* installed on your system?

If you can't run the script, please visit the following URL and follow the instructions there:

https://pygobject.readthedocs.io/en/latest/getting_started.html

People who've just switched from Windows will also need to run:

sudo apt-get install python3-pyqt5

to install PyQt5.

Everyone will also need version 1.x of Gstreamer:

sudo apt-get install gstreamer1.0-tools

sudo apt-get install gstreamer1.0-plugins-ugly

Now you're all set for the next part.

8.2. Gstreamer

Back when I was in grade school, classes on Friday used to end at 3:20 pm. I'd usually end up at my friend Mo's house. His dad was a mechanic and had all sorts of cool hardware that I liked going through while he was still at work. My folks had dull office jobs and their work things weren't worth going through.

One day we discovered an electronics puzzle kit among his dads things. We could make simple circuits by snapping puzzle pieces together to match patterns shown in a book that accompanied the kit. I'd always loved radio and we followed the instructions to assemble a simple crystal radio. I was cynical about the claim that one could make a radio without any electricity and wasn't surprised when it didn't work. Mo read the instructions through again and we spent half an hour fiddling with a water tap before we got it to work.

It turned out that we'd assembled it correctly, but we hadn't grounded it. There was a faint signal on the earphones from a local AM station, but it worked. Each puzzle piece had an electric circuit component soldered underneath it as well as connectors on either side that joined to other circuit components. It was quite complex for 10-year old kids without any electronics training, but the pictures on top of the puzzle pieces made it look and feel like a game. Search Amazon for "Snap Circuits". What we used was similar, but wasn't as colorful as today's models.

Gstreamer is similar to those snap circuits. It comes with various components, that you can assemble together to make many different multimedia tools like a DVD player, streaming Internet radio player and recorder etc. The team that won the 2016 Nobel Prize for Physics used a Gstreamer plugin to help them detect gravity waves. If you have a Samsung flat-screen TV or have watched a movie on an airplane, they were probably using Gstreamer.

I will not give a comprehensive tutorial on Gstreamer(consult their website for that, links in the references section), I only give you an overview that will allow you to follow the code for this chapter. If you're not technically-inclined, you can think of this like building a puzzle(like me and Mo did) and not worry too much about what's beneath the puzzle pieces you're assembling.

8.2.1. Pipeline

The substrate or puzzle board on which all puzzle pieces(elements) are mounted is called the pipeline. Elements process the data(for example output from your favorite Internet radio site) as it moves downstream from the source elements, to sink elements(like your speaker) passing through filter elements. Playing media straight from the Internet without storing it locally is known as streaming.

Figure 8.2. Image courtesy of gstreamer.freedesktop.org

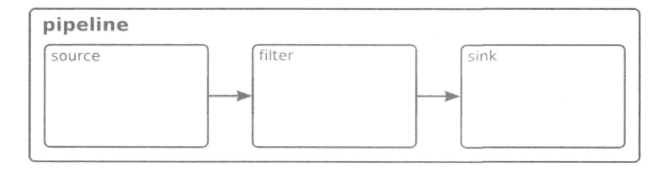

8.2.2. Elements

The ports through which GStreamer elements communicate with each other are called pads. There exists sink pads, through which data enters an element, and source pads, through which data exits an element. It follows naturally that source elements only contain source pads, sink elements only contain sink pads, and filter elements contain both. Source pads produce data, sink pads consume data.

Figure 8.3. Data flows "down" the pipeline from left to right (image courtesy of gstreamer.freedesktop.org)

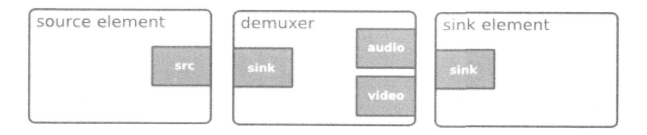

A demultiplexer for digital media files, or media demultiplexer also called a file splitter by laymen or consumer software providers, is software that breaks down individual elementary streams of a media file, e.g., audio, video, or subtitles and sends them to their respective decoders for actual decoding. A media file for example an mp4 file is a container that has several streams of data packed together. An mp4 player will be able to read and unpack these streams of audio, video and subtitles in a process called decoding, then present them to you in a coherent manner, directing output to your speakers and video screen.

Media demultiplexers are not decoders themselves, but are format container handlers that separate program streams from a file and supply them to their respective audio, video, or subtitles decoders. A demuxer contains one sink pad, through which the muxed data arrives, and multiple source pads, one for each stream found in the container.

A pipeline for a basic ogg player is illustrated below:

Figure 8.4. Image courtesy of gstreamer.freedesktop.org

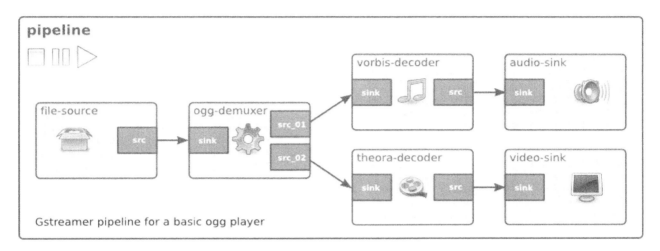

Ogg is an open source file format. To confirm that you have a working version of Gstreamer tools installed on your system, run the following command:

gst-launch-1.0 videotestsrc ! autovideosink

This will open a window with a video test pattern on your system. If the above command run successfully, try the following command:

gst-launch-1.0 audiotestsrc ! autoaudiosink

This will generate a 440 Hz audio test tone. Switch on your speakers to confirm that it works. Next we're going to combine the audio and video in one pipeline and output the result as an ogg file. Type in:

gst-launch-1.0 audiotestsrc ! vorbisenc ! oggmux name=mux ! filesink location=file.ogg videotestsrc ! theoraenc ! mux.

and let it run for at least 30 seconds.

You can terminate it by pressing *Ctrl+C*. This will output 30 seconds of data into a file called *file.ogg*. Inspect your current working directory and confirm that this file exists!

Most of the above command should be familiar to you. Specifying the "name" property of an element lets you use it more than once. We take the output of the audio test source, feed it into an ogg muxer and name it *mux*. We then use *mux* again, by feeding the output of a video test source into it. Finally, we take the combined result and direct it into a file named *file.ogg*.

Remember, muxing is packing several streams of data for example audio, video and subtitles into a single container file. In effect what we've done is take Figure 8.4 above and run it from right to left.

8.2.3. Pads

Pads are an element's interface to the outside world. Data streams from one element's source pad to another element's sink pad. In addition to direction of data flow, pads have another important property- availability.

A pad can have any of three availabilities: always, sometimes and on request. The meaning of those three types is exactly as it says: always pads always exist, sometimes pad exist only in certain cases (and can disappear randomly), and on-request pads appear only if explicitly requested by applications. For this basic introduction, we will ignore request pads.

Some elements might not have all of their pads when the element is created. This can happen, for example, with an Ogg demuxer element. The element will read the Ogg stream and create dynamic pads for each contained elementary stream (vorbis, theora) when it detects such a stream in the Ogg stream. Likewise, it will delete the pad when the stream ends.

On your CLI run the following:
gst-inspect-1.0 oggdemux
and inspect the output.

The element has only one pad: a sink pad called "sink". The other pads are "dormant". You can see this in the pad template because there is an "Exists: Sometimes" property. Depending on the type of Ogg file you play, the pads will be created. We will see that this is very important when you are going to create dynamic pipelines. You can attach a signal handler to an element to inform you when the element has created a new pad from one of its "Sometimes" pad templates.

8.2.4. Element states

After being created, an element will not actually perform any actions yet. You need to change an elements' state to make it do something. GStreamer knows four element states, each with a very specific meaning. These four states are:

1. GST_STATE_NULL: this is the default state. No resources are allocated in this state, so, transitioning to it will free all resources. The element must be in this state when its reference count reaches 0 and it is freed.

2. GST_STATE_READY: in the ready state, an element has allocated all of its global resources, that is, resources that can be kept within streams. You can think about opening devices, allocating buffers and so on. However, the stream is not opened in this state, so the stream position is automatically zero. If a stream was previously opened, it should be closed in this state, and position, properties and such should be reset.

3. GST_STATE_PAUSED: in this state, an element has opened the stream, but is not actively processing it. An element is allowed to modify a stream's position, read and process data and such to prepare for playback as soon as state is changed to PLAYING, but it is not allowed to play the data which would make the clock run. In summary, PAUSED is the same as PLAYING but without a running clock.

    Elements going into the PAUSED state should prepare themselves for moving over to the PLAYING state as soon as possible. Video or audio outputs would, for example, wait for data to arrive and queue it so they can play it right after the state change. Also, video sinks can already play the first frame (since this does not affect the clock yet). Autopluggers could use this same state transition to already plug together a pipeline. Most other elements, such as codecs or filters, do not need to explicitly do anything in this state, however.

4. GST_STATE_PLAYING: in the PLAYING state, an element does exactly the same as in the PAUSED state, except that the clock now runs.

You can change the state of an element using the function *set_state()*. If you set an element to another state, GStreamer will internally traverse all intermediate states. So if you set an element from NULL to PLAYING, GStreamer will internally set the element to READY and PAUSED in between.

8.2.5. Bringing it all together

Is your head spinning after that whirlwind tour through Gstreamer? It's time to bring it all together with a simple PyQt example that will reinforce what you've learnt so far. In the folder for this chapter open a file named *baby.py*. We will programmatically implement Illustration 25 and you will get to see an example of dynamic pipelines in action.

Run the following command:

python3 baby.py

Click on the start button, this will open a file selection dialog. Select the ogg file we created in the previous section. It will automatically start playing. You can stop it by clicking "Stop" in the main window. For this simple player, only start and stop states are possible. The next section will explain how it works.

Figure 8.5. First screen of your player

Figure 8.6. Select the file you created in the last section

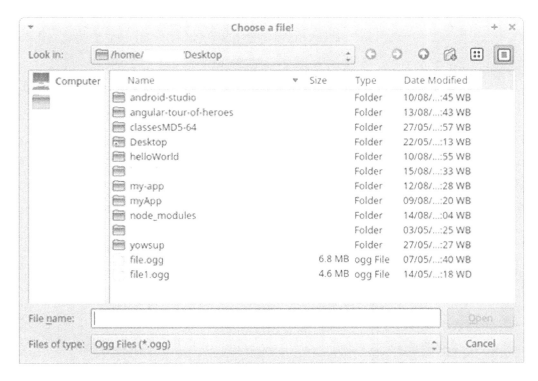

Figure 8.7. The file is automatically played

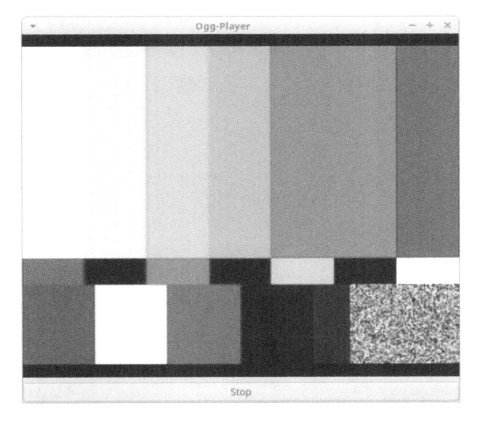

8.2.6. Explanation of the code

First we'll cover the U.I. setup.

Most Gstreamer scripts will have lines 2 to 5. They ensure that Gstreamer 1.x is installed on the system before the script runs. You've encountered a vertical box layout in a previous chapter. Lines 19 and 20 create an instance of one here and set it to occupy the entire area of the window. Its internal widgets will expand to occupy as much space as possible(which is why the button looks kind of stretched). We use a QOpenGLWidget widget on line 22. We will redirect our videosink output into this widget. This widget inherits from the QWidget class. This is important for us because we need to pass the window id of this widget to our videosink.

```
1  import sys
2  import gi
3  gi.require_version('Gst', '1.0')
4  gi.require_version('GstVideo', '1.0')
5  from gi.repository import Gst, GstVideo
6  from PyQt5.QtWidgets import QApplication, QWidget, QPushButton, QFileDialog, QOpenGLWidget, QVBoxLayout
7
8  class MainWindow(QWidget):
9      def __init__(self):
10         super().__init__()
11         self.initUI()
12         self.initPlayer()
13
14     def initUI(self):
15         self.setWindowTitle('Ogg-Player')
16         self.resize(546, 475)
17         self.setGeometry(0, 0, 546, 475)
18
19         self.verticalLayout = QVBoxLayout(self)
20         self.verticalLayout.setContentsMargins(0, 0, 0, 0)
21
22         self.openGLWidget = QOpenGLWidget(self)
```

Now we look at the basic gstreamer setup flow.

Before you do anything, you must initialize Gstreamer. Line 33 is another line that all Gstreamer scripts I've seen have. Lines 34-36 create a pipeline. We then create file-source and demuxer elements. These will be linked together in our pipeline later. The elements on each path are created in lines 43-49. Did you notice the two extra elements that aren't in Figure 8.4? The script will probably run just fine without *audioconv* and *videoconv*. According to the Gstreamer documentation, these extra elements are necessary to guarantee that the pipeline can be linked. The capabilities of the audio and video sinks depend on the hardware, and you do not know at design time if they will match the capabilities produced by the audio and video test sources. If the capabilities match, these elements act in "pass-through" mode and do not modify the signal, having negligible impact on performance. After we've created all the elements of our pipeline, we bring them together as shown on lines 51-61. Lines 63-70 link the elements on each path together.

```
33 def initPlayer(self):
34   Gst.init(None)
35   self.player = Gst.Pipeline.new("player")
36   source = Gst.ElementFactory.make("filesrc", "file-source")
37   demuxer = Gst.ElementFactory.make("oggdemux", "demuxer")
38   demuxer.connect("pad-added", self.demuxer_callback) 🯱
39
40   self.queuea = Gst.ElementFactory.make("queue", "queuea") 🯲
41   self.queuev = Gst.ElementFactory.make("queue", "queuev") 🯳
42
43   self.audio_decoder = Gst.ElementFactory.make("vorbisdec", "vorbis-decoder")
44   audioconv = Gst.ElementFactory.make("audioconvert", "convertera")
45   audiosink = Gst.ElementFactory.make("autoaudiosink", "audio-output")
46
47   self.video_decoder = Gst.ElementFactory.make("theoradec", "theora-decoder")
48   videoconv = Gst.ElementFactory.make("videoconvert", "converterv")
```

```
49  videosink = Gst.ElementFactory.make("autovideosink", "video-output")
50
51  self.player.add(source)
52  self.player.add(demuxer)
53  self.player.add(self.audio_decoder)
54  self.player.add(audioconv)
55  self.player.add(audiosink)
56  self.player.add(self.queuea)
57
58  self.player.add(self.video_decoder)
59  self.player.add(videoconv)
60  self.player.add(videosink)
61  self.player.add(self.queuev)
62
63  source.link(demuxer)
64  self.queuea.link(self.audio_decoder)
65  self.audio_decoder.link(audioconv)
66  audioconv.link(audiosink)
67
68  self.queuev.link(self.video_decoder)
69  self.video_decoder.link(videoconv)
70  videoconv.link(videosink)
71
72  bus = self.player.get_bus()  ❹
73  bus.add_signal_watch()  ❺
74  bus.connect('message', self.on_message)  ❻
75  bus.enable_sync_message_emission()  ❼
76  bus.connect("sync-message::element", self.on_sync_message)  ❽
```

❶ As mentioned earlier, a pad can have 3 capabilities. An oggdemux element has "sometimes" capabilities. Depending on the data fed into it, it will create dynamic pads for each stream it finds. Since we're using the file we created earlier, the *demuxer_callback()* function will be called twice for each stream contained in our file.

2 **3** Have a look at Figure 8.4 again! The output from the demuxer is directed down two separate paths, one for audio another for video. The audio output in our program will be represented by *self.queuea*, while the video will be represented using *self.queuev*.

4 **5** The pipeline transmits signals when it's in different states. For example if we come to the end
6 of a playing file, a stop notification will be emitted. Or if there's an error we can print out some debug information and gracefully exit.

7 **8** This is for the video output. A "prepare-window-handle" message will be sent from the video sink. We set up a listener for this message and specify an action to take when we receive a message.

So far so good. The main obstacle we'll face is directing the output to the appropriate devices. Gstreamer "needs" to know where to send the video output. Every *QWidget* object has a window id property. We get this and pass it to Gstreamer.

Please examine lines 79-90! We need to pick a file to pass to our file-source element. We open a file selection dialog and filter it to only accept files with the ".ogg" extension. Once we find such a file, we change the pipeline to the PLAYING state and change the button label to "Stop". The else case on line 88, resets the pipeline if we stop a playing stream. Have a look back at lines 63 and 64. Did you notice we didn't link our demuxer to our queue elements? The demuxer output depends on the input data presented to it. Sometimes it may only have audio output, other times video or even text output. When it has output, a new pad is created. The code that handles this is shown on lines 92-102. Lines 93-95 query the output of a new pad. If it has either output of type audio or video, we connect it to the appropriate queue for further processing. Signal handling code is usually the same on many Gstreamer projects. The code that does this is on lines 104-113. Events are all put on a queue. We listen for two events- EOS(End of Stream) and ERROR. In case of EOS, we set the player button text back to "Start", showing that it's ready to receive new input. Setting the pipeline to null, frees all resources consumed by it. When the ERROR event is fired, we print an error and prepare to receive more input. Line 115-119 define the handler we set up on line 76. We direct output to our videosink, show it the window to use for its output and specify that it should maintain its aspect ratio.

```
78 def start_stop(self):
79    if self.button.text() == 'Start':
80      filepath = QFileDialog.getOpenFileName(self,"Choose a file!", "","Ogg Files (*.ogg)")
```

```
81    #filepath returns a tuple containing ('/home/yourpathhere/yourfilenamehere.ogg', 'Ogg Files (*.ogg)')
82    #we need to unpack this tuple to obtain a filename we can use
83    #filepath[0] is a string containing the filename we want for example /home/yourpathhere/yourfilenamehere.ogg
84    if filepath:
85      self.button.setText('Stop')
86      self.player.get_by_name("file-source").set_property("location", filepath[0])
87      self.player.set_state(Gst.State.PLAYING)
88    else:
89      self.player.set_state(Gst.State.NULL)
90      self.button.setText('Start')
91  
92  def demuxer_callback(self, demuxer, newpad):
93   res = Gst.Pad.get_current_caps(newpad)
94   structure = Gst.Caps.get_structure(res, 0)
95   result = Gst.Structure.get_name(structure)
96   if "audio" in result:
97    print(result)
98    adec_pad = self.queuea.get_static_pad("sink")
99    newpad.link(adec_pad)
100  if "video" in result:
101   vdec_pad = self.queuev.get_static_pad("sink")
102   newpad.link(vdec_pad)
103  
104 def on_message(self, bus, message):
105   t = message.type
106   if t == Gst.MessageType.EOS:
107     self.player.set_state(Gst.State.NULL)
108     self.button.setText('Start')
109   elif t == Gst.MessageType.ERROR:
110     self.player.set_state(Gst.State.NULL)
111     err, debug = message.parse_error()
```

```
112     print('Error: %s' % err, debug)
113     self.button.setText('Start')
114
115 def on_sync_message(self, bus, message):
116   if message.get_structure().get_name() == 'prepare-window-
handle':
117     videosink = message.src
118     videosink.set_property("force-aspect-ratio", True)
119     videosink.set_window_handle(self.openGLWidget.winId())
```

8.3. Radio app

We finally get to the radio app. This app incorporates Gstreamer to stream data from an Internet radio station. It has a beautiful U.I. that incorporates PyQt elements to provide a lot of the functionality you'd expect from a media-player and then some. In this section we'll only focus on the PyQt code. From the CLI run the following command:

python3 qt5radio.py

If everything is set up correctly you should see the following:

Figure 8.8. Our radio app

Unlike many radio players, this one allows you to record what you listen to as an mp3 file. This time we'll focus on the U.I. part of the app.

After loading the icons, we set the default radio station from our database on line 45. Lines 50-54 demonstrate how to set button icons.

```
45 self.station=radio_db[0][0]
46 self.old_title=""
47
48 # Source for icons
49 # https://icons8.com/icon/set/media-player/all
50 self.app_icon=QIcon(icons_dir+"/audio-wave-64.png")
51 self.play_icon=QIcon(icons_dir+"/play-64.png")
52 self.stop_icon=QIcon(icons_dir+"/stop-64.png")
53 self.rec_icon=QIcon(icons_dir+"/downloads-64.png")
54 self.mute_icon=QIcon(icons_dir+"/mute-64.png")
```

Line 16 reads from a file containing a list of radio stations and stores the result in a variable named *radio_db*. Lines 74 to 76 populate our combobox with all the entries in our radio station database. On line 77 we set up an event handler which is called anytime we access the combobox. Even if we don't change the station, as long as we click on the combobox this event handler will be called.

```
71 def initUI(self):
72   label = QLabel("Radio station: ", self)
73
74   combo = QComboBox(self)
75   for i in radio_db:
76     combo.addItem(i[0])
77   combo.activated[int].connect(self.onActivated)
```

This is the event handler triggered when we access the combobox. If the radio is currently playing, it is stopped. The index of whichever item is selected on the combobox is looked up in our radio database and passed to our Gstreamer component, ready to be streamed. The log component in line 165, refers to the non-editable textbox you can see in Figure 8.8. We also change the main window title, every time we change stations.

```
151 def onActivated(self, idx):
152   # when changing station, do the following
153   # 1. stop playing old station
```

```
154  # 2. switch to new station
155  # 3. play new station
156
157  # 1. If playing, stop playing
158  self.stop()
159
160  # 2. Swtich to new station
161  #self.pipeline.set_state(Gst.State.NULL)
162  self.station=radio_db[idx][0]
163  self.setWindowTitle(radio_db[idx][0])
164  self.http_source.set_property("location", radio_db[idx][1])
165  self.log.appendPlainText("%s: Switch to station %s"
166      % (time.asctime(time.localtime()),
167         self.station))
```

We set up our play button. We pass a "1" or True to several of its attributes like *setDefault* and *setCheckable*. *SetDefault* is what makes it look darker than the others, like its just been pressed. s*etCheckable* allows us to interact with it. Clicking on uncheckable buttons doesn't trigger any events. We then set its event handler and icon.

```
79  self.playBtn=QPushButton(self)
80  self.playBtn.setDefault(1)
81  self.playBtn.setCheckable(1)
82  self.playBtn.setIcon(self.play_icon)
83  self.playBtn.resize(self.playBtn.sizeHint())
84  self.playBtn.clicked.connect(self.onPlay)
```

Lines 172-173 link the play button to its event handler whose code is shown below. After toggling some variables, it sends a GST_STATE_PLAYING to our pipeline.

```
220  self.playBtn=QPushButton(self)
221  self.playBtn.setDefault(1)
222  self.playBtn.setCheckable(1)
223  self.playBtn.setIcon(self.play_icon)
224  self.playBtn.resize(self.playBtn.sizeHint())
225  self.playBtn.clicked.connect(self.onPlay)
```

Lines 175-176 link the stop button to its event handler whose code is shown below. Its event handler sends a GST_STATE_NULL message to our pipeline. This stops anything that's playing and frees internal resources.

```
227 def stop(self):
228   self.playing=0
229   self.playBtn.setChecked(0)
230   self.stopBtn.setChecked(1)
231   self.pipeline.set_state(Gst.State.NULL)
232   self.mainloop.quit()
```

Lines 92-96 link the record button to its event handler whose code is shown below. The event handler checks to see if its already recording. If it is, it stops. It it's not recording and a stream is playing, it begins the recording process. It it's not recording and a stream isn't playing an error message is produced.

```
178 def onRec(self):
179   if self.recording:
180     self.log.appendPlainText("%s: Recording stop"
181         % (time.asctime(time.localtime())))
182     self.filesink.set_state(Gst.State.NULL)
183     self.filesink.set_property("location", "/dev/null")
184     self.filesink.set_state(Gst.State.PLAYING)
185     self.recording=0
186   else:
187     if self.playing:
188       now=time.strftime("%y%m%d_%H%M%S")
189       self.log.appendPlainText("%s: Recording started"
190           % time.asctime(time.localtime()))
191       self.filesink.set_state(Gst.State.NULL)
192       self.filesink.set_property("location", "%s_%s.mp3" %
193           (now, self.station))
194       self.filesink.set_state(Gst.State.PLAYING)
195       self.recording=1
196     else:
197       self.log.appendPlainText("Recording not started. " +
```

```
198               "No playing stream")
199     self.recBtn.setChecked(0)
```

Lines 102-106 link the mute button to its event handler whose code is shown below. In order to mute all we need to do is set the mute property of the audio sink.

```
201 def onMute(self):
202   if self.muteBtn.isChecked():
203     self.play_audio.set_property("mute", 1)
204   else :
205     self.play_audio.set_property("mute", 0)
```

Lines 108-111 link the volume slider to its event handler whose code is shown below. Its event handler sends the audio sink an appropriate signal depending on the current state as well as user input.

```
207 def onVolChanged(self, event):
208   pos=self.volCtrl.sliderPosition()
209   self.play_audio.set_property("volume",
 self.volMultiple*pos/100.0)
210   #print(self.play_audio.get_property("volume"))
211   if pos==0:
212     self.muteBtn.setChecked(1)
213     self.play_audio.set_property("mute", 1)
214   else:
215     self.muteBtn.setChecked(0)
216     self.play_audio.set_property("mute", 0)
217   #if self.volCtrl.event(QEvent.MouseButtonPress):
218   QToolTip.showText(QCursor.pos(), "%d" % pos, self)
```

The code below sets up the log window.

```
 98 self.log=QPlainTextEdit()
 99 self.log.setReadOnly(1)
100 self.log.setWordWrapMode(0) # No text wrap
```

8.4. Summary

Aren't you glad you took the time to understand a bit about how Gstreamer works? Your basic knowledge combined with what you already know about PyQt, has enabled you to understand a fairly complex application, such as what you'd encounter in the real world.

Understanding how the non-Qt part of the projects you'll encounter in the real world interacts with the Qt part of the code, will often be the main challenge you face as a Qt developer.

8.5. References

- https://en.wikipedia.org/wiki/GStreamer

- https://www.slideshare.net/DuncanMacleod4/detecting-gravitational-waves-in-python

- https://gstreamer.freedesktop.org/documentation/application-development/basics/elements.html#element-states

- https://gstreamer.freedesktop.org/documentation/application-development/basics/pads.html#dynamic-or-sometimes-pads

- https://doc.qt.io/qt-5/qmainwindow.html#setCentralWidget

- https://gstreamer.freedesktop.org/documentation/design/messages.html

- https://doc.qt.io/qt-5/qcombobox.html#activated

- https://doc.qt.io/qt-5/qabstractbutton.html

- https://github.com/kelvintan/qt5radio

- https://doc.qt.io/qt-5/qwidget.html

- https://doc.qt.io/qt-5/qwidget.html#winId

- https://brettviren.github.io/pygst-tutorial-org/pygst-tutorial.html

Appendix A: Multi-threading

Open the directory called "A" in the "Appendix" folder and run *thread-demo.py*.

Figure A.1. Threads demo

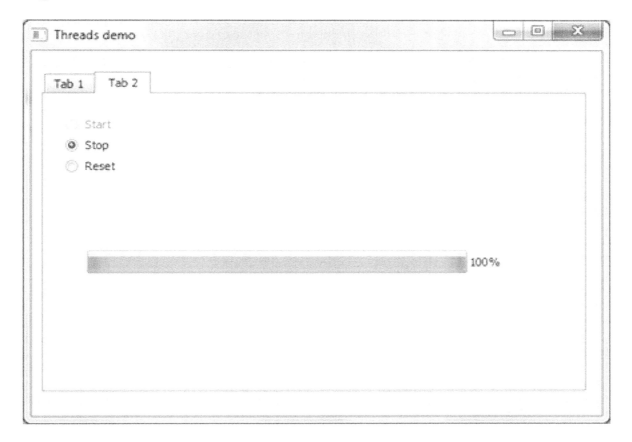

Ideally, you should be able to click start, have the progressbar slowly shift to 100% and it should stop when you click the "Stop" radio button. This doesn't happen though, try it for yourself and see. Once you click "Start" you have to wait for the progressbar to reach 100% before you can do anything else. You can't even switch tabs and the script appears to hang if you try to interact with it, as it ticks away to 100.

Why does this happen? Perhaps you've encountered something similar in your scripts or in other people's scripts. This occurs because execution flow is stuck inside the while loop shown in line 60 of *thread-demo.py*. By default, there is only one single thread running and everything else stops until the while loop completes.

To see the contrast, un-comment line 65 and run the script again. This time, you can stop the progressbar bar midway. And you can interact with other components for example, switching tabs as the progressbar ticks away. This time, the while loop is contained in a separate thread from the rest of the script logic.

What is a thread? A Thread or a Thread of Execution is defined in computer science as the smallest unit that can be scheduled in an operating system. Threads are normally created by a fork of a computer script or program into two or more parallel (which is implemented on a single processor by multitasking) tasks. Threads are usually contained in processes. More than one thread can exist within the same process. These threads share the memory and the state of the process. In other words, they share the code or instructions and the values of its variables.

There are two different kinds of threads:

- Kernel threads

- User-space threads or user threads

Kernel threads are part of the operating system, while User-space threads are not implemented in the operating system kernel.

Every process has at least one thread, i.e. the process itself. A process can start multiple threads. The operating system executes these threads like parallel "processes". On a single processor machine, this parallelism is achieved by thread scheduling or time slicing. Looking back at our above example, instead of having to wait for the while-loop to finish, we can fork a parallel execution flow to deal with other user input processing.

However, it's important to note that threads only appear to be running in parallel. Python implements the Global Interpreter Lock(GIL), which prevents threads from running in parallel(even on multi-processor computers). Through task-switching, Python rapidly switches between many tasks and gives the illusion of parallel processing.

Threading can useful in applications that have a lot of downtime as they wait for user input or even network input.

A.1. How to implement threading

We've seen one way to implement this as shown in line 65, by using *Qapplication.processEvents()*. However, this is only a stopgap measure and should only be used occasionally when our script program is performing a long operation. For Qt programming, we will use the *QThread* class for our multi-threading needs.

The generic structure of a threaded app is as follows:

```
1  from PyQt5 import QtCore
2
3  class YourThreadName(QtCore.QThread):
4
5      def __init__(self):
6          super(YourThreadName, self).__init__(parent)
7
8      def run(self):
9          # your logic here
```

QThread is a simple class that you can pass arguments to when creating a new instance since it has a normal init method. Also, when you want to run the thread, you don't call the *run()* method itself, you call *start()* instead. Calling *run()* directly in some cases can freeze your main thread depending on how the run method is implemented in your thread.

In the code for *thread-demo-final.py* an argument is passed to the new instance. This argument contains the initial value for the progressbar. The thread is initialized and started as shown:

```
77 self.runThread = RunThread(parent=None,
counter_start=start_value)
78 self.runThread.start()
```

 Tip

In Qt, we have an alternative to the callback technique: we use signals and slots. A signal is emitted when a particular event occurs. Qt's widgets have many predefined signals, but we can always subclass widgets to add our own signals to them. A slot is a function that is called in response to a particular signal. Qt's widgets have many pre-defined slots, but it is common practice to subclass widgets and add our own slots so that you can handle the signals that you are interested in.

```
76     def progressbar_counter(self, start_value=0):
77         self.runThread = RunThread(parent=None,
counter_start=start_value)
78         self.runThread.start()
```

```
79        self.runThread.counter_value.connect(self.set_progressbar)
80
81        def set_progressbar(self, counter):  ❷
82            if not self.stopProgress:
83                self.progressBar.setValue(counter)
84
85    class RunThread(QtCore.QThread):
86
87        counter_value = QtCore.pyqtSignal(int)  ❸
88
89        def __init__(self, parent=None, counter_start = 0):
90            super(RunThread, self).__init__(parent)
91            self.counter = counter_start
92            self.isRunning = True
93
94        def run(self):
95            while (self.counter < 100) and (self.isRunning == True):
96                sleep(0.1)  ❹
97                self.counter += 1  ❺
98                print(self.counter)  ❻
99                self.counter_value.emit(self.counter)  ❼
100
101       def stop(self):
102           self.isRunning = False
103           print("Stopping Thread")
104           self.terminate()
```

❶   This line initializes our thread and then calls its *run()* method on line 94.

❹ ❺ After sleeping briefly, we update our counter value and print out a debug value.

❻

❼   This emits a signal and its listener, that is, the slot that listens for the particular event was created on line 79.

2 This function is called every time our thread emits a signal. Basically what this does is increment by 1% the value of the progress bar. Approximately every tenth of a second, the progress bar value will increase slightly.

3 So far, we've only provided slots to connect to ready-made signals. This is how you create a signal and you *emit* its value as shown on line 99. Line 87 creates a signal that emits an integer argument.

A.2. References

- https://www.python-course.eu/threads.php

- https://en.wikipedia.org/wiki/Global_interpreter_lock

- https://doc.qt.io/qt-5/qcoreapplication.html#processEvents

- https://doc.qt.io/qt-5/signalsandslots.html

- https://doc.qt.io/qt-5/qthread.html

This page intentionally left blank

Appendix B: Network Access Manager

In the chapter where we designed the currency exchange rates app, we used the *requests* module to communicate with a web service. It was intuitive and pretty easy to use. However, Qt also comes with its own network communication class called *QNetworkAccessManager*. Using it has one major advantage namely, it provides us with signals that we can use with other Qt widgets.

The Network Access API is constructed around one *QNetworkAccessManager* object, which holds the common configuration and settings for the requests it sends. It contains the proxy and cache configuration, as well as signals related to such issues and reply signals that can be used to monitor the progress of a network operation. One *QNetworkAccessManager* instance should be enough for the whole Qt application. Since *QNetworkAccessManager* is based on *QObject*, it can only be used from the thread it belongs to.

Once a *QNetworkAccessManager* object has been created, the application can use it to send requests over the network. A group of standard functions are supplied that take a request and optional data, and each return a *QNetworkReply* object. The returned object is used to obtain any data returned in response to the corresponding request.

The code below is found in *get.py*.

```
 5  class MainWindow(QObject):
 6      def __init__(self):
 7          super().__init__()
 8
 9          target = "http://pyqt.sourceforge.net/Docs/PyQt5/index.html"  ❶
10          request = QNetworkRequest(QUrl(target))
11
12          self.networkAccessManager = QNetworkAccessManager()  ❷
13          self.networkAccessManager.finished.connect(self.onFinished)  ❸
14          self.networkAccessManager.get(request)  ❹
15
```

```
16     def onFinished(self, response): #response is an object of type QNetworkReply
17         error = response.error() 5
18
19         if (error == QNetworkReply.NoError): 6
20             result = response.readAll() # you can print this if you like 7
21             print("Response content type is: "+response.header(QNetworkRequest.ContentTypeHeader)) 8
22             print("Server response time is: "+response.header(QNetworkRequest.LastModifiedHeader).toString()) 9
23         else:
24             print("There was an error. "+response.errorString())
25
26         self.windUp(response) 10
27
28     def windUp(self, replyObject): #replyObject is an object of type QNetworkReply
29         print("Network request completed!")
30         replyObject.deleteLater() 11
31         QCoreApplication.quit()
32
33
34 if __name__ == '__main__':
35
36     qApp = QCoreApplication(sys.argv) 12
37     w = MainWindow()
38     sys.exit(qApp.exec_())
```

1   The *QNetworkRequest* class holds a request to be sent with *QNetworkAccessManager*. *QNetworkRequest* is part of the Network Access API and is the class holding the information necessary to send a request over the network. It contains a URL and some ancillary information that can be used to modify the request.

2 3   We initialize our *QNetworkAccessManager* object. We pass it the *QNetworkRequest* object it
4   will use and connect a slot which will be called after the request is completed.

5	We are inside the slot which means the network request is complete. Once the request is complete, Qt hands us back a response object of type *QNetworkReply*. We take our response and check it for errors.
6 7 8 9	This block executes if our network request completes successfully. We stored the resulting response in a variable called *result* and then we print out some server response headers. Have a look at line 18 again. *response.header(QNetworkRequest.LastModifiedHeader)* returns an object of type *QDateTime*. To convert this into an easy to read format, we call the *toString()* method of *QDateTime*.
10	This line calls the *windUp()* method.
11	According to the PyQt documentation(https://doc.qt.io/qt-5/qnetworkaccessmanager.html#details), we must delete the *QNetworkReply* object after we finish with it. We do this by calling the *deleteLater()* method of our object.
12	Note that we're using *QCoreApplication* instead of *QApplication* like we've previously done. *QCoreApplication* is used to create PyQt applications that don't have a GUI. Just like GUI PyQt applications, they have one primary thread and may have any number of secondary threads.

B.1. References

- https://doc.qt.io/qt-5/qnetworkrequest.html#details

- https://doc.qt.io/qt-5/qnetworkrequest.html#KnownHeaders-enum

- https://doc.qt.io/qt-5/qnetworkaccessmanager.html#details

- https://doc.qt.io/qt-5/qnetworkrequest.html#details

This page intentionally left blank

Appendix C: Setting up Cygwin

This section will walk you through installing cygwin on your Windows PC. Most of the scripts in the book can be run using cygwin, but, a few will not work as well as expected.

C.1. Initial setup

Figure C.1. The website

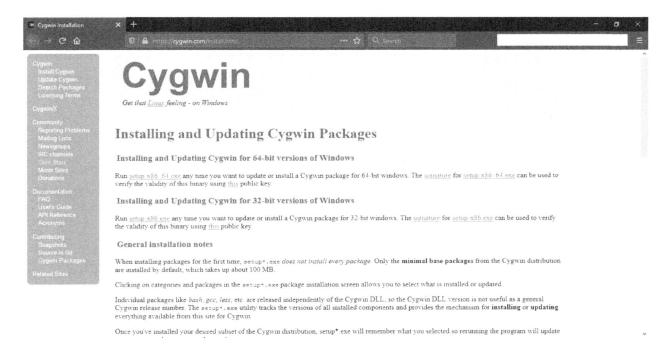

Go to the cygwin website and download the appropriate binary for your system. I'm running on a 64-bit system, so I chose *setup-x86_64.exe*

Store the file you download in an easy-to-remember location.

Important

Do not delete the binary you download from the cygwin website! Even after the initial setup, this file will be used to install additional packages, as well as for updating your current setup.

Execute the file on a computer connected to the Internet. It will ask you to select a download mirror. If you're in doubt about which to choose, use the default.

Figure C.2. Mirror selection

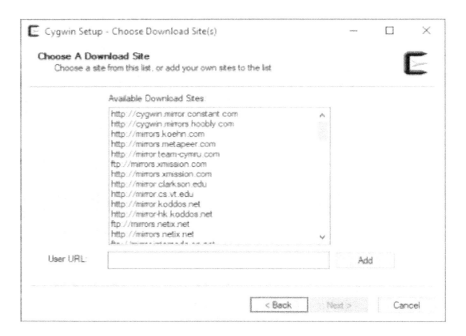

Keep clicking *Next* just like in a typical setup wizard. It will download the files, expand them and install to your system.

C.2. Your first package

The default Cygwin subsystem runs from the command line. In order to run PyQt scripts, we need to set up a graphical user interface. Remember the binary you downloaded from the cygwin site? You need to run this to setup X Windows on cygwin.

It will go through many of the steps from the initial setup. After downloading some information from a mirror, it will pause at the following stage as it waits for user input.

Figure C.3. Setup awaiting user input

Click the dropdown menu and select *Not Installed* as shown below.

Figure C.4. Narrow down your choices

Appendix C: Setting up Cygwin   126

Many packages you've not installed will show up. We want to narrow our search down. Type *xinit* into the search text box.

Figure C.5. Choose the latest version

We will have two packages to choose from. Select the latest version of xinit and click the next button. After downloading the required packages, it will setup X Windows on cygwin. Sometimes you will get a post-install error message similar to the one shown below.

Figure C.6. Error message

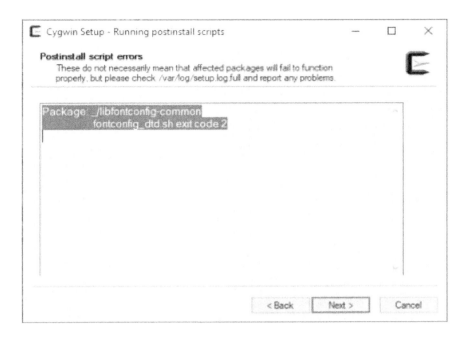

Don't worry about this. Everything will still work.

C.3. Run the system for the first time

After adding xinit, your Start menu will look similar to the following.

Appendix C: Setting up Cygwin   128

Figure C.7. Start menu after installing xinit

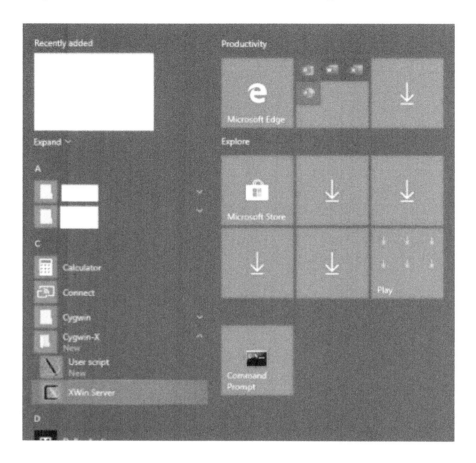

Click the highlighted menu entry. In the bottom right of your taskbar, click the following icon.

Figure C.8. Run this program

From the popup menus, select *System Tools>XTerm*.

This will open a terminal window similar to the one shown below.

Figure C.9. All GUI scripts should be run in this terminal

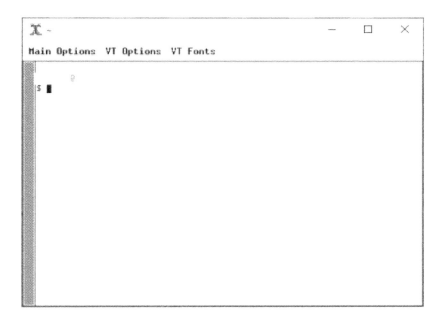

When invoked from this terminal, any PyQt script that has a GUI will run in its own separate window.

C.4. Installing additional packages

Congratulations! You've set up your first package. All additional packages will be setup similarly.

 Important

Please note that additional packages you install will not show up in the Start menu like the xinit package did.

To verify that you've installed a package, run the binary you downloaded from the cygwin site and keep clicking next till you get to the input screen like before. Select *Up To Date* from the dropdown menu and type the name of the package in the input text box. An example with the xinit package is shown below.

Appendix C: Setting up Cygwin130

Figure C.10. Confirm the installation of a package

Packages installed in the cygwin subsystem will show up here. For the PyQt scripts to run, you will need to install additional packages. If you get any errors, use the above procedure to confirm that you've installed the appropriate package.

C.5. Packages to run basic scripts

If you switch to the scripts directory and try to run a script now, you will get several errors. Python3 isn't even installed yet. To remedy this, repeat the install procedure outlined above and search for a package named *python3-pyqt5*.

Figure C.11. Set up PyQt

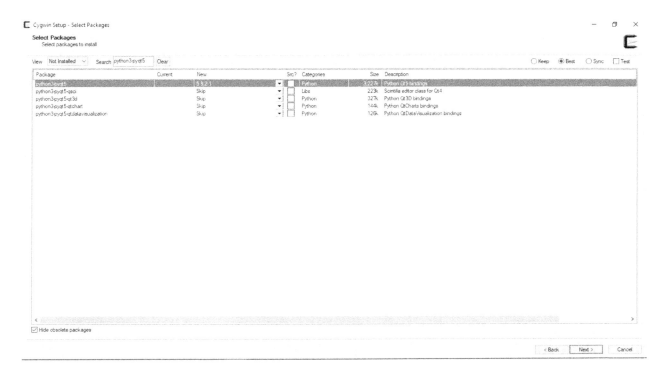

After the setup completes, Python3 will be installed on your system. If you try to run a script now, you will get an error message:

ModuleNotFoundError: No module named 'sip'

Repeat the install process and install a package named *python3-sip*. After installing it, you will be able to run *simple.py* in the folder for the first chapter. I had to maximise and minimise a few times before the window loaded properly.

Figure C.12. The basic app

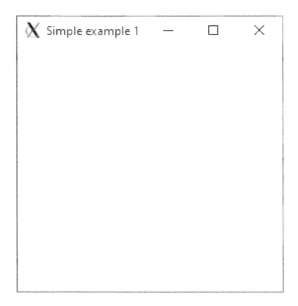

C.6. OpenGL packages

The next hurdle you will encounter will be with the 5th example in the widgets chapter. When you run the script you will get the following error message:

Figure C.13. OpenGL error

To remedy this, install the latest version of *python3-opengl*. I had to enlarge and restore the application window to its original size before it run properly.

Figure C.14. widget5.py

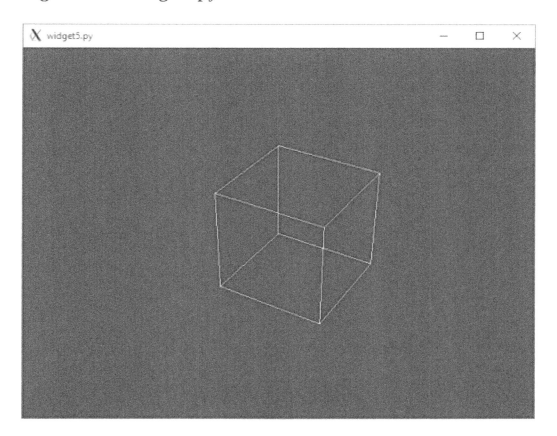

C.7. Radio app

The largest hurdle you will encounter will be in the radio app chapter. If you try to run *hello.py* you will receive an error message:

ValueError: Namespace Gtk not available

Install the following packages:

- *python37-gi*

- *gobject-introspection*

- *gstreamer1.0*

- *gstreamer1.0-python*

- *gstreamer1.0-plugins-ugly-free*

Appendix C: Setting up Cygwin   134

- *python-gtk2.0*

- *girepository-Gtk3.0*

The script will then run successfully.

Figure C.15. Basic GTK setup on cygwin

To run the CLI commands as well as the other apps, install the following packages:

- *gst123*

- *girepository-GstInterfaces1.0*

Figure C.16. Radio app on cygwin

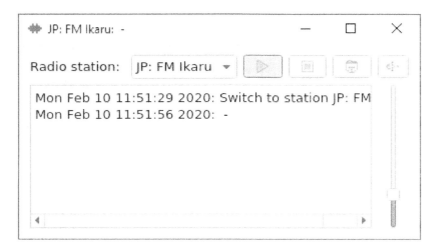

As mentioned before, performance on cygwin may be suboptimal, but if you have no alternatives…

Made in the USA
Monee, IL
02 January 2022